Great Rock 'n' Roll Street Art

Victor Burleigh

Schiffer Publishing Ltd

4880 Lower Valley Road, Atglen, PA 19310 USA

Designed by John P. Cheek
Type set in Korinna BT

ISBN: 0-7643-2099-8
Printed in China

Published by Schiffer Publishing Ltd.
4880 Lower Valley Road
Atglen, PA 19310
Phone: (610) 593-1777; Fax: (610) 593-2002
E-mail: Info@schifferbooks.com

For the largest selection of fine reference books on this and related subjects, please visit our web site at
www.schifferbooks.com
We are always looking for people to write books on new and related subjects. If you have an idea for a book please contact us at the above address.

This book may be purchased from the publisher.
Include $3.95 for shipping.
Please try your bookstore first.
You may write for a free catalog.

In Europe, Schiffer books are distributed by
Bushwood Books
6 Marksbury Ave.
Kew Gardens
Surrey TW9 4JF England
Phone: 44 (0) 20 8392-8585;
Fax: 44 (0) 20 8392-9876
E-mail: info@bushwoodbooks.co.uk
Free postage in the U.K., Europe; air mail at cost.

Introduction

In the 1980s, in cities across the land, it was not uncommon to wake up in the morning and find nearly every telephone pole sporting a poster advertising some event or concert. Looked at in retrospect, these posters make up a kind of "street art," with all the vitality and creativity of the youth culture. Mostly produced on photocopiers or simple litho printers, the designs were avant garde, raw, and powerful in order to catch the eye of passers-by.

San Francisco was at the heart of the punk rock phenomenon. Nearly every night one of the clubs, including the *Mabuhay Gardens, On Broadway, The Farm, I-Beam, Nightbreak,* and many more, would offer a live concert of an up-and-coming group.

Mabuhay Gardens was the biggest punk rock club in San Francisco and was also known as "the Fab Mab." It started as a supper club, offering live shows after 8pm. *On Broadway* was upstairs and had many shows for all ages. *The Farm* was a petting zoo during the day and featured live bands at night. As you went downstairs you could smell the zoo. The *I-Beam* was an upstairs club on Haight Street with two bars. It was so popular that there was usually a line five or six people deep just to order a drink! *Nightbreak* started as Speedway Records and evolved into a full time bar.

With live shows every night, these clubs and many others around the bay area had so many great bands that sometimes it was hard to decide which show to see, and when you chose where you wanted to go you would have to shove your way through the crowds. Some of the bands went on to national prominence, while others drew a large following in the Bay Area and other venues on the West Coast, from Seattle to Los Angeles.

To advertise the shows the clubs would make posters for each concert and post them by the hundreds on every available spot, poles, blank walls, coffee shops, and in the clubs. Though usually unnamed and limited by the simple printing media, the artists who produced these posters created "in your face" graphics that caught the eye at a glance.

This is a collection of nearly 750 of these original posters, produced from 1977 to 1989. They were "liberated" from the street (you can often see the staple holes in them) and lovingly cared for as a record of an era. They reveal a wide range of styles and graphic images, as well as a history of the rock scene in the 1980s.

The author's thanks goes out to all the bands and venue owners, for many years of great live music for all these years.

MONDAY AUGUST 10
KUSF/KALX CO-PRESENT
FLIPPER
the DEAD MILKMEN
MR T EXPERIENCE
DOORS 9pm
SHOW 10pm

I BEAM

1748 HAIGHT ST.
ADVANCE TIX AT I-BEAM, REVOLVER, HALL OF RECORDS
ROUGH TRADE, RECKLESS, AQUARIUS & BASS
MONDAY AUGUST 17 : NEW MODEL ARMY ● POISON 13

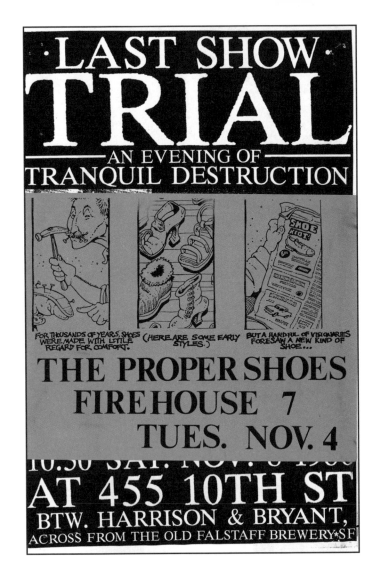

·LAST SHOW·
TRIAL
AN EVENING OF
TRANQUIL DESTRUCTION

FOR THOUSANDS OF YEARS, SHOES WERE MADE WITH LITTLE REGARD FOR COMFORT.
(HERE ARE SOME EARLY STYLES.)
BUT A HANDFUL OF VISIONARIES FORESAW A NEW KIND OF SHOE...

THE PROPER SHOES
FIRE HOUSE 7
TUES. NOV. 4
10.30 SAT. NOV. 8 1986
AT 455 10TH ST
BTW. HARRISON & BRYANT,
ACROSS FROM THE OLD FALSTAFF BREWERY*SF

Denim TV

FRIDAY OCT. 11
Full Moon Saloon - 11pm
1725 Haight st.- SF

night break
THE WITNESSES
EARLY SHOW
MAY
12
THURSDAY
with
CARNIVAL LAW

4

The Keystone Family Invites You to

Celebrate The New Year With

CHRIS ISAAK

New Years' Eve Party
Thursday December 31, 1987
with

PAUL COLLINS' BEAT

$25.00 *includes complimentary champagne and party favors*

Friday January 1, 1988
with

THE SORENTINOS

$10.00/11.50

THE STONE   412 Broadway   San Francisco   (415) 391-8282

Both shows doors open 8 PM   18 and older admitted   21 and older for complimentary champagne
on New Years' Eve   Advance tickets available through all BASS outlets.

5

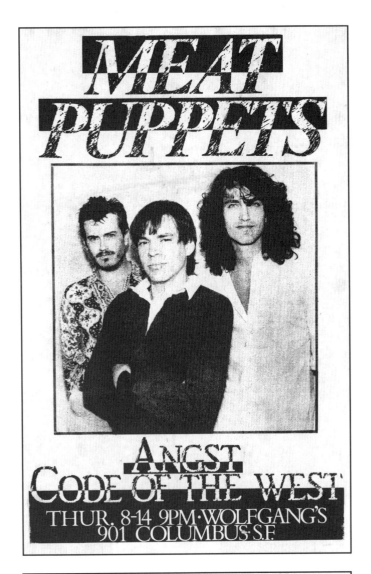

MEAT PUPPETS

ANGST
CODE OF THE WEST
THUR. 8-14 9PM·WOLFGANG'S
901 COLUMBUS·S.F.

THE SCREAMIN' SIRENS 4-29
THE DOOR SLAMMERS 4-30
TUES & WED APRIL 29 & 30 8 PM

Wolfgang's
901 Columbus Avenue • San Francisco • 474-2995

TIX AT ALL BASS OUTLETS

PLUS SPECIAL GUEST

TUES AUG 26 9PM

Wolfgang's
901 Columbus Avenue • San Francisco • 474-2995

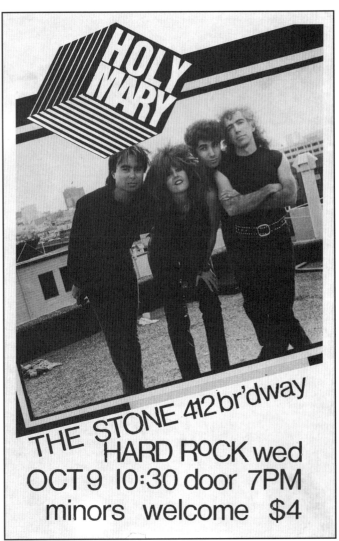

THE STONE 412 br'dway
HARD ROCK wed
OCT 9 10:30 door 7PM
minors welcome $4

VOMIT LAUNCH
THINKING FELLERS UNION 282
WORLD OF POOH
Social life of pederasts
THURSDAY NOVEMBER 19 9 PM
SF MUSIC WORKS
CHURCH AND MARKET

WORLD OF POOH
WITH THESE DAYS
SUNDAY APRIL 10 6 PM
SF MUSIC WORKS
CHURCH AND MARKET

BOMB
Record Release Party for BOMB
TRAGIC MULATTO
COTTON BREAK
San Francisco Music Works – April 8, 1988
This party won't cost any money but there is a necessary donation:
one hat or one unopened pack of cigarettes (Marlboro or Export "A" Light)
per person. Thank you. The first fifty people will get a free record too.

TUE MARCH 29 9pm
The Devils
& MISSILE HARMONY
SF MUSIC WORKS
BEWARE! the DEVILS ON PREMISES
21 PLUS ID

7

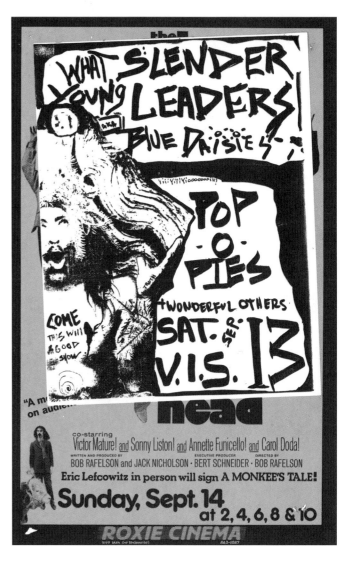

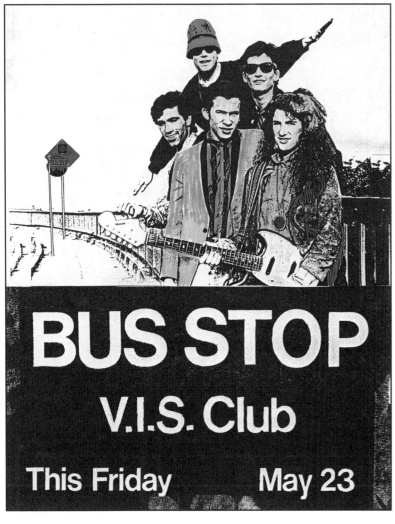

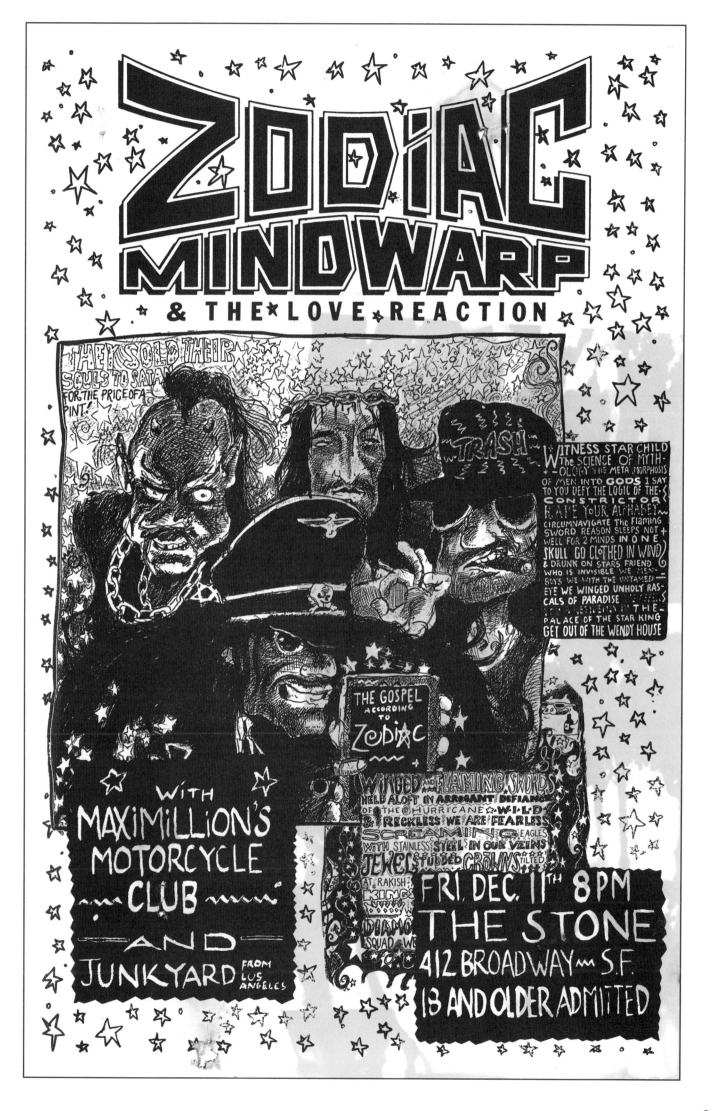

9

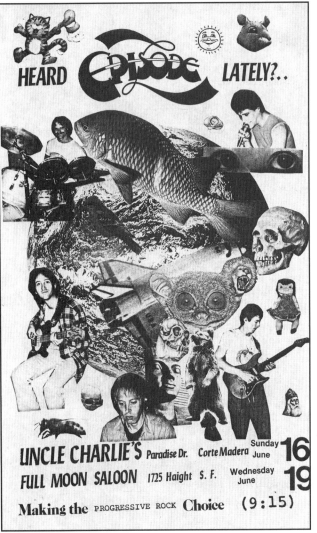

helios Creed .... from hell

the BAGS ...from Boston

steel pole bath tub
...from nowhere in particular

MONDAY APRIL 4TH 930

S.F. MUSIC WORKS [861-7484]

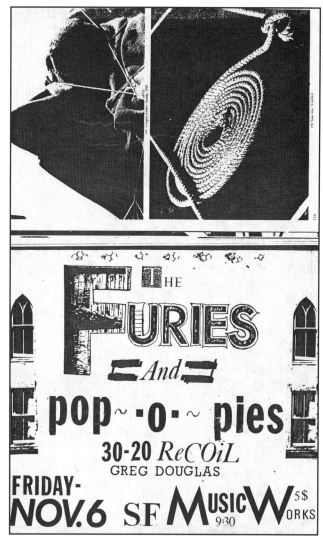

THE FURIES And pop~·o·~ pies

30-20 ReCOiL
GREG DOUGLAS

FRIDAY-
NOV. 6   S.F. MUSIC WORKS
9:30   5$

PENELOPE HOUSTON
BIRDBOYS

NOV 18 MUSIC WED WORKS

crawl away machine
lives

full moon saloon
wed. the 13th- 9:00

11

SISTER DOUBLE HAPPINESS

RECORD RELEASE PARTY!

MONDAY, FEB 22

plus from los angeles
JUNKYARD
YO LA TANGO

I BEAM
1748 HAIGHT ST. (AT COLE)

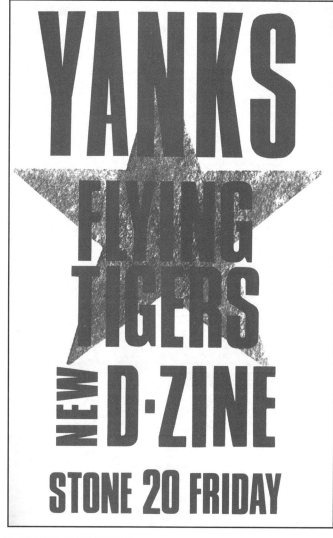

YANKS
FLYING TIGERS
NEW D-ZINE
STONE 20 FRIDAY

RAGE OF EDEN
theStone
Fri Feb 13 with THE NUNS

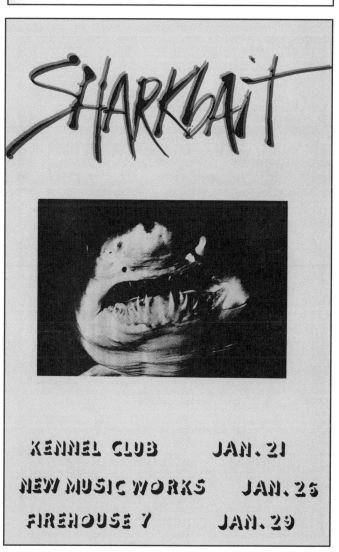

SHARKBAIT

KENNEL CLUB   JAN. 21
NEW MUSIC WORKS   JAN. 25
FIREHOUSE 7   JAN. 29

13

LIVE URBAN **DANCE** LIVE URBAN **DANCE**
9th ~THURS.~ All Night   9th ~THURS.~ All Night

JANUARY   JANUARY

TOO MUCH FUN   TOO MUCH FUN

A THE
FULL MOON
SALOON
1725 HAIGHT STREET

A THE
FULL MOON
SALOON
1725 HAIGHT STREET

The
STONE S.F.
WELCOMES

AMARANTH

ADVANCE TIX: $5.00   NIGHT OF SHOW: $7.00

DEDICATED ROCKER!!

THURSDAY AUGUST 7, 1986   DOORS OPEN 8:00 pm
                                 SHOW STARTS AT 9:00 pm

ERUPTION
PRODUCTIONS
MANAGEMENT
(408) 241-9239

18 AND OVER WELCOME

B. TAVEN

WOLFGANG'S ROAD SHOW PRESENTS

the

BoDEANS

Hard Rain

City Nights

715 Harrison St., S.F.

Monday, November 16 at 9 pm

Tickets at BASS   All ages Welcome

S.F. MUSIC WORKS

LOOK ER THERE

THURSDAY 10 PM

MAY 26

14

15

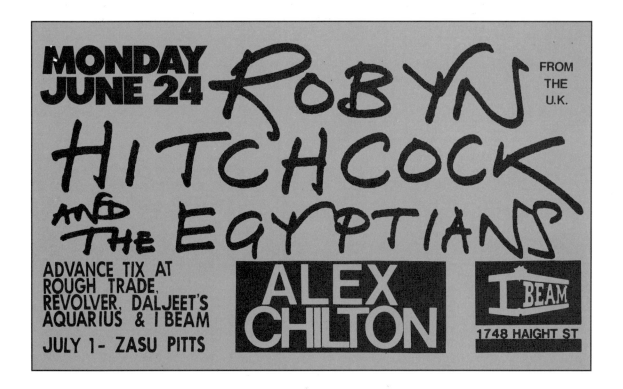

MONDAY JUNE 24 ROBYN HITCHCOCK AND THE EGYPTIANS

FROM THE U.K.

ADVANCE TIX AT ROUGH TRADE, REVOLVER, DALJEET'S AQUARIUS & I BEAM

JULY 1- ZASU PITTS

ALEX CHILTON

I BEAM
1748 HAIGHT ST.

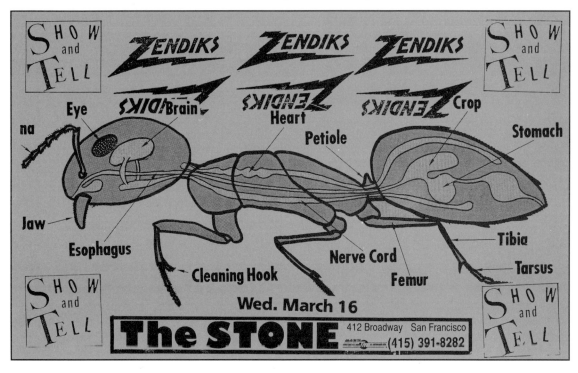

SHOW and TELL

ZENDIKS ZENDIKS ZENDIKS

Eye Brain Heart Crop
na Petiole Stomach
Jaw
Esophagus Nerve Cord Tibia
Cleaning Hook Femur Tarsus
Wed. March 16

The STONE 412 Broadway San Francisco (415) 391-8282

MON. MAY 20 dream syndicate

KUSF/BAM/KALX CO-PRESENT
A BAY AREA EXCLUSIVE

JUNE 3- BILLY BRAGG

EDDIE RAY PORTER'S STATE OF THINGS
(FEAT. CHUCK PROPHET OF GREEN ON RED)

I BEAM
1748 HAIGHT ST

17

VIVI • SECTION

THURS

OCT. 13
8-11 pm

$ three
A.T.A.
922 VALENCIA

THE GIRL WHO'S NEVER BEEN KISSED:

Pennsylvania Mahoney

AND HER
SAFE SEXTET
• • •
THE FINAL FLING!

PENNY'S LAST

PERFORMANCE

BEFORE GOING ABROAD!

★

FRI.
JUL. 1

FREE
FREE

PARADISE
LOUNGE
11ª/FOLSOM

4 PRESENTS:

FREE BOWL
OF CLOWN POOP
WITH TEN
COUPONS!

the amazing fantastic amazing

SPOT
10 19

WAR

and: the inimitable

NICE
GUYS

FOUR BUCKS
AND WORTH
EVERY CENT

PEACE

oh but wait that's not
all! It's those wild and wiggly

WRESTLING
WORMS

all together again 'at last' for the first time

SAT. JULY 19

9:00 PM

better get there early if you
don't want to miss the wet t-shirt
and boxer shorts contest

at the beautiful
CLUB FOOT
3rd st. at 22nd (NEXT TO "FRIENDLY"
BUS STOP LIQUORS)

PLUS: FILMS
BY J. SWANSON,
M. SULLIVAN and
"OTHERS"

Fade To Black

AN ENDLESS NIGHT

MAY
25

ROZZ AND JEFF
A READING BY JULIA DAWN
GRAFFITI

ALCOHOLOCAUST presents a HAPPY HOUR SHOW
with
DEAD AND GONE
THE PHANTOM LIMBS

FRI. NOV. 3RD
show starts 6 PM
$3 · 21 & over

COVERED WAGON SALOON
911 FOLSOM @ 5TH ST. SAN FRANCISCO

45 GRAVE

FrightWig & Wages of Sin

SAT MAY 9

431·1326

MABUHAY
443 BROADWAY
S.F.

GONE WORLD

saturday

NOV 23

Vis

SVT

SYMPTOMS

AUGUST 18
9:00

SAVOY
1438 GRANT AVE

AMC

THE WANKERS

SAT. MAY 11
HOTEL UTAH

YOU ARE INVITED TO A BENEFIT PARTY for the MANIC D. PRESS. featuring CATHEADS BLUE MOVIE vs. THE FURIES CLUBFOOT 3RD + 22ND STS., S.F. SAT. NOV 16 9 p.m. $3.00

CLUB FOOT ORCHESTRA
Polkacide
SAT MAR 23
chi chi club
440 Broadway, S.F.   392-6213

22

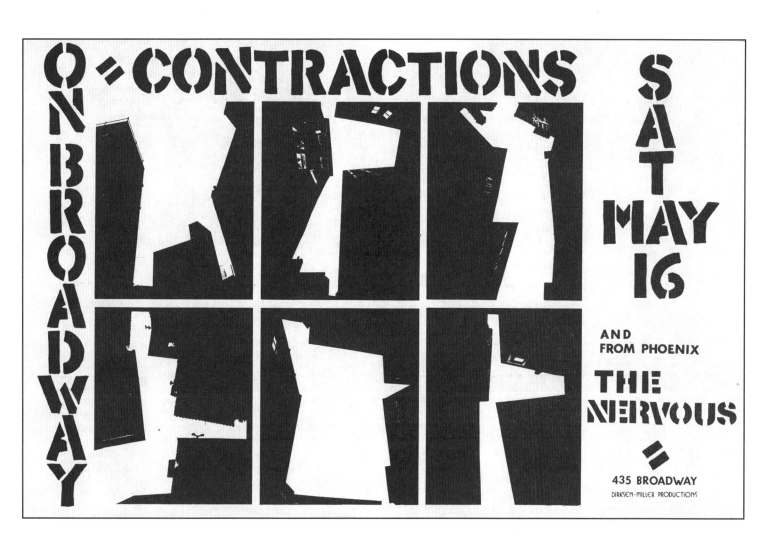

ON BROADWAY
= CONTRACTIONS
SAT MAY 16
AND FROM PHOENIX
THE NERVOUS
435 BROADWAY
DIRKSEN-MILLER PRODUCTIONS

CONTRACTIONS
VARVE
WILMA
FRIDAY JUNE 5 MABUHAY GARDENS

TUESDAY APRIL 28
EARLY SHOW!
KUSF/KALX CO-PRESENT

THE FLESHTONES

DOORS 8pm
SHOW 9pm

I BEAM
1748 HAIGHT ST.

ADVANCE TIX AT I-BEAM, REVOLVER, HALL OF RECORDS
ROUGH TRADE, RECKLESS, AQUARIUS, DALJEETS & BASS

MONDAY MAY 4: THE MEKONS

LABOR DAY WEEKEND
MCMLXXXV

SOUND OF MUSIC
162 Turk St., S.F.

MABUHAY GARDENS
443 Broadway, S.F.

Friday, August 30
11:00 P.M.

Sunday, September 1
Midnight

The return of
MY SIN
In June

Friday 14 _____ Nightbreak
Saturday 15 _____ Mabuhay
(Minors ok)
Saturday 22 _____ Vis a Vis
(Record release party)

New 12"EP **Beyond Good** *available June 20*
And Evil

D N A
LOUNGE

BLACKLIGHT
CHAMELEONS
Final S.F. Performance

Wed. July 22
Doors 9:00 PM
$5.00

Followed By "COLD SWEAT"
Dancing with Dj Adam Fisher
Midnight to 4 AM

21 & OLDER PLEASE HAVE I.D.
375 11th Street 626-1409

28

KNEW 91 & PARADISE PRODUCTIONS

Presents

"California Country Harvest"

* * * * * * * * *

Proceeds Benefit

The Farm

Starring

New Riders Of The Purple Sage

Lynn Edgar Beadles   Jessica James

& the California Country All Stars

SUNDAY
October 26th 1986
(2 pm til 8 pm)

at

Tickets & Information (415 621-1003)

THE FARM
1499 Potrero Avenue
IN San Francisco

- $6 Per Person
$10 Per Couple
Kids Free!

A DIVISION OF PEACE, INC.

DAS BLOK 17 WED JUNE MAB

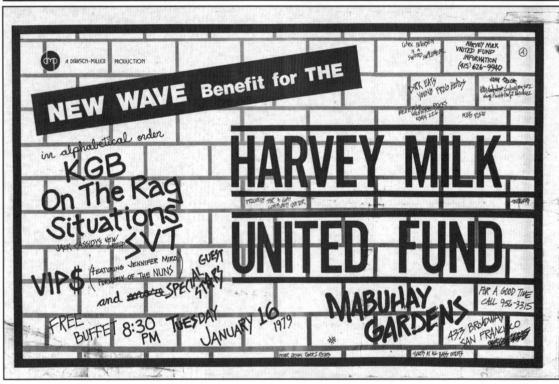

dmp A DIRKSEN-MILLER PRODUCTION

DICK PETERSEN IS A SWORD SWALLOWER

HARVEY MILK UNITED FUND INFORMATION (415) 626-9940 ④

DICK EATS YOUNG FROG HEADS

JOHN DELOR

BEVERLY WILSHIRE ROCKS KSAN 226

NUNS RULE

NEW WAVE Benefit for THE

in alphabetical order

KGB
On The Rag
Situations
SVT (JACK CASSIDY'S NEW GROUP)

VIP$ (FEATURING JENNIFER MIRO, FORMERLY OF THE NUNS) and SPECIAL GUEST STARS

HARVEY MILK

UNITED FUND

FREE BUFFET 8:30 PM TUESDAY JANUARY 16 1979

Mabuhay Gardens

FOR A GOOD TIME CALL 956-3315

433 BROADWAY SAN FRANCISCO

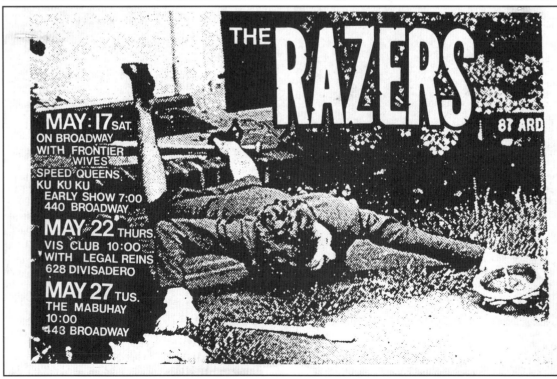

THE RAZERS
87 ARD

MAY 17 SAT.
ON BROADWAY
WITH FRONTIER WIVES
SPEED QUEENS
KU KU KU
EARLY SHOW 7:00
440 BROADWAY

MAY 22 THURS.
VIS CLUB 10:00
WITH LEGAL REINS
628 DIVISADERO

MAY 27 TUS.
THE MABUHAY
10:00
443 BROADWAY

PAN-IDIOMATIC FESTIVAL

"I once spent the night at his house, and when I woke up, I saw Monk at the piano composing while the radio on top of the piano was blasting away, playing hillbilly music."   His manager has recalled:

THE INVERTEBRATES
TERRA-INCOGNITA &

SAT. JULY 6, 9:30 $3

SPINELESS RECORDS

CLUB FOOT

2520 3RD ST S.F. CA, 94107

glam slam
Proudly Presents

Speed Queens

I wish I had a big cock just like Iggy Pop

At

Hotel Utah
4th & Bryant
SAN·FRANCISCO.

SATURDAY
9 NOV

INFO
421·8308

CLUB FooT
Fri. MAY 17
Moraly BANKRUPT
BUrning Witches
CRASH-N-BURN
AND
TYPHOON

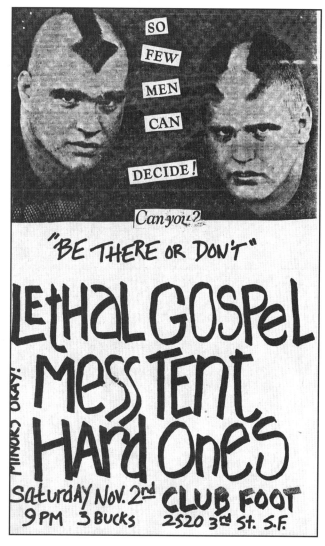

SO
FEW
MEN
CAN
DECIDE!

Can you?

"BE THERE OR DON'T"

MINORS OKAY!

LEtHal GOSPeL
MeSS TeNT
HaRd OneS

Saturday Nov. 2nd   CLUB FOOT
9 PM 3 Bucks   2520 3rd St. S.F.

31

Thur. 27
RADWASTE

NIGHT BREAK

Wed. 26
700 CLUB

Sat. 29 'YO

THIS SATURDAY

GREG KIHN

CIRCLE STAR THEATRE
MAY 25 1985 8PM $12.50

TICKETS AT ALL BASS OUTLETS

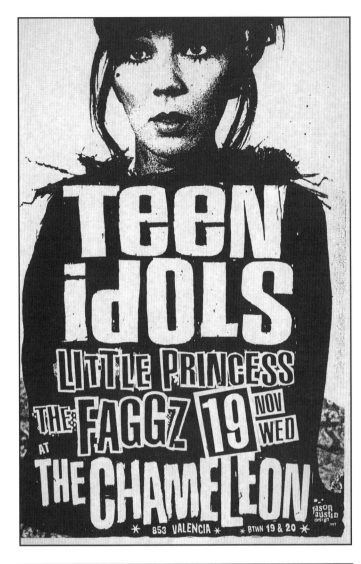

TEEN idOLS
LITTLE PRINCESS
THE FAGGZ
AT THE CHAMELEON
19 NOV WED
★ 853 VALENCIA ★ BTWN 19 & 20 ★
jason austin design 1997

CONTRACTIONS
ROCK OUT APRIL TOUR - 81

Photo: F Stop Fitzgerald ©1980

KANTNER BALIN CASADY BAND
WITH
STICK AGAINST STONE

FRIDAY, MAY 16th 8:00 PM

THE FARM

1499 POTRERO (Near Army), S.F. 826-4290 $8.00 ADVANCE $10.00 DOOR

AVAILABLE AT BASS TICKET CENTERS

34

OPEN 1 PM - 11 PM

SPEEDWAY RECORDS

OPENING SATURDAY JAN. 30

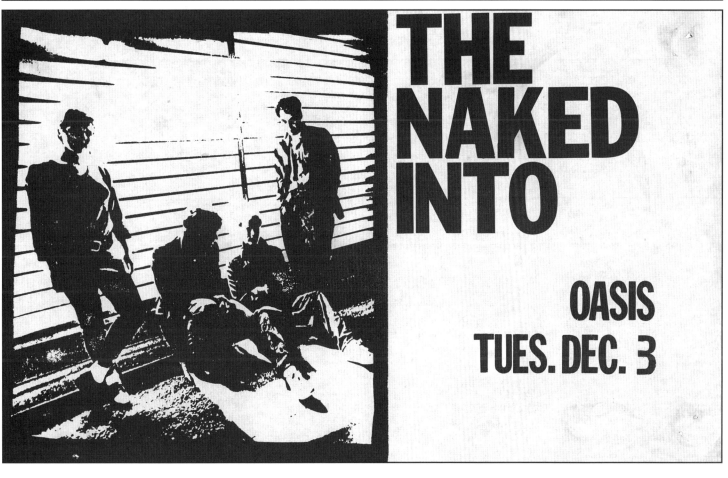

THE NAKED INTO

OASIS
TUES. DEC. 3

DENIM T.V.

PROGRAM   GUIDE

MAY 5 NIGHTBREAK 5 PM
9 MABUHAY GARDENS
30 GRAFFITI
(live on KUSF 90.3 fm)

PSYCHIC ORPHINS
REOPENING NOW
KU KU KU
THE MAB
THURS JUNE 12
$1.00 BEER ALL NIGHT
FREE FOOD
$3.00 AT DOOR
SIVA DANCING
BROTHER HOOD OF LIGHT

the DONNER PARTY

WEDNESDAY night, THE FIRST day of MAY, NO one CARES

at the: FAB MaB past bedtime

•ALSO•
in the east at:

two days before CINCO de MAYO

RUTHIE'S with flying color ←

MusiKcamp

Mabuhay
442 B'way
WED MAY 15

36

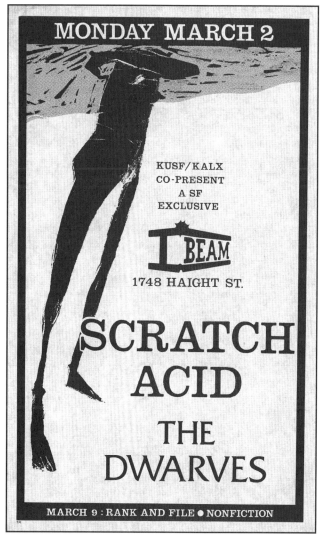

COMIC BOOK OPERA

RECORD RELEASE SHOW

SHIVA DANCING

NIGHTBREAK

FRI JUN 10TH

DOORS OPEN 7:30

the Farm

July 4th

Flipper
Sea Hags
Sister Double Happiness
Housecoat Project
Board of Mackeral
O TYPE

Crossroads Community
1499 Potrero Avenue
San Francisco, CA 94110

July 11th
Capitol Punishment
Fang
Verbal Abuse
Social Unrest
Victim's Family
State of Confusion (from Idaho)
Dehumanizers (from Seattle)
Special Forces
Mr. T. Experience
Neurosis

PRE-HANGOVER IN THE SUN SHOW

Thursday August 23rd

ENDLESS STRUGGLE
From Utah

KONTRAKLASSE
From L.A.

From San Francisco

BORN DEAD
From Oakland

From L.A.

Blattant Riddicule
From Santa Cruz

CLIT 45

7$ all ages 7 p.m. sharp!!!!

at Burnt Ramen Studios 111 Espee ave. in Richmond

DIRECTIONS: FROM BAY BRIDGE 80 TO 580 TOWARDS RICHMOND SAN RAFAEL BRIDGE FROM 580 EXIT 23rd GO RIGHT / GO LEFT #110 / GO RICH AT 20th / THEN RIGHT AT CHANSELOR / BURNT RAMON ON CORNER / 111 ESPEE AVE -N- CHANSELOR

MARHAY GARDENS
A DIRKSEN-MILLER PRODUCTION
VS

- WITH -
Neutrinoz
Witnesses
No Alternative
and G'est
Laguerre
with Tommy Savage

10 pm
Sun MAR 9

Lou Rudolph '90

LETHAL DOSE
FROM SANTA BARBARA CA

LAST U.S. SHOW BEFORE THE EUROPEAN TOUR IN MAY

RKL

Food will be catered but you should ...donations needed & gladly accepted Bring Your Own Whatever...

12-3 PM FREE! APRIL 23 SAT

at the unbelievable..........

GOLDEN G. PARK BANDSHELL!!

FREE SHOW
SAT 23rd 12:00 NOON

THE BLASTERS

SCREAMIN' SIRENS

PLUS SPECIAL GUESTS

WED. JULY 31 9 PM
KABUKI
1881 POST ST. SF
TIX AT ALL BASS OUTLETS

JIM CARROL
CASUAL
ITALIANS
6/26/87
MAB
10 PM   Friday

JET BOY
oct.31
7pm On
broadway
433 broadway s.f.
all ages

a benefit party for
high frontiers magazine

the morlocks

black athletes

code of the **west**

vicious hippies

kor phu

a neopsychedelic
coming-out party

dec. 7   pearl harbor day
1 p.m. - 1 a.m. $10
the farm 1499 potrero, s.f.

Wiring Dept. Magazine Benefit
Sunday, October 12

FLAMING LIPS
RHYTHM and NOISE
GLORIOUS DIN
RAINING HOUSE
PLATEAU ENSEMBLE
WEDNESDAY MORNING,
3 A.M.

$5 — From 7 to 12:30
ALL AGES WELCOME
THE FARM 1499 POTRERO

Fade To Black
MY SIN

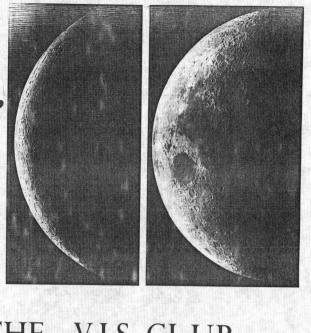

SATURDAY
NOV. 9

THE VIS CLUB
628 DIVISADERO
WITH
SHIVA DANCING

KFJC presents at CLUB VIS -620 Divisadero-

PALMETTO STATE
KOr-PHU.
CAMPER Von BEETHOVEN
TUES. AUG. 6

RRZ Presents at the ON BROADWAY
THEATRE NIGHTCLUB
398-0800

Thurs. Dec. 2
Social Distortion
Toxic Reasons
Articals of Faith
Urban Assault

Fri. Dec. 10
Pop-O-Pies

Sat. Dec. 11
D.O.A.
Crucifix
Don't miss this one!

Thurs. Dec. 16
T.S.O.L.

Sat. Dec. 18 & Sun. Dec. 19
BLACK FLAG
and Guest
Christmas was never like this!

Fri. Dec. 10
LYDIA LUNCH
Plus Pop-O-Pies

CRUCIFIX
nineteen eighty-four

THE 2nd ANNUAL
HELLFIRE CLUB
WITH LIVE ONSTAGE
OUR LADY OF PAIN
DANCE TO YOUR DEATH
+ ALTER DEFEY
BODY NIGHTCLUB & MORE
THURSDAY JULY 18th
Mabuhay Gardens
443 BROADWAY SF
A PAGAN RITUAL PRODUCTION

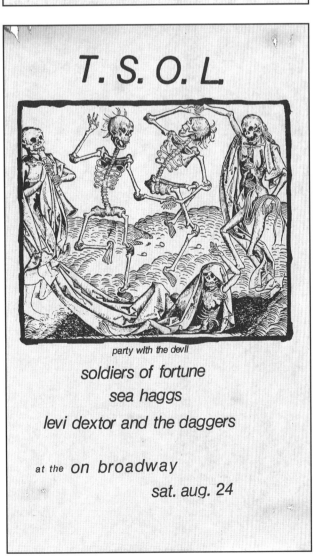

T.S.O.L

party with the devil

soldiers of fortune

sea haggs

levi dextor and the daggers

at the on broadway

sat. aug. 24

ASSASSIN
with...
WATCHTOWER
HEADLINING
+ cronic Plague
saturday · oct. 4
7:00 pm
rock on
broadway
8:00
ADVANCE TIX:
753-2047
421-3523
$9.00 AT THE DOOR

THE SEAHAGS
Friday NIGHT
AUGUST Fourteenth
The KENNEL Klub
628 DIVISADERO sf

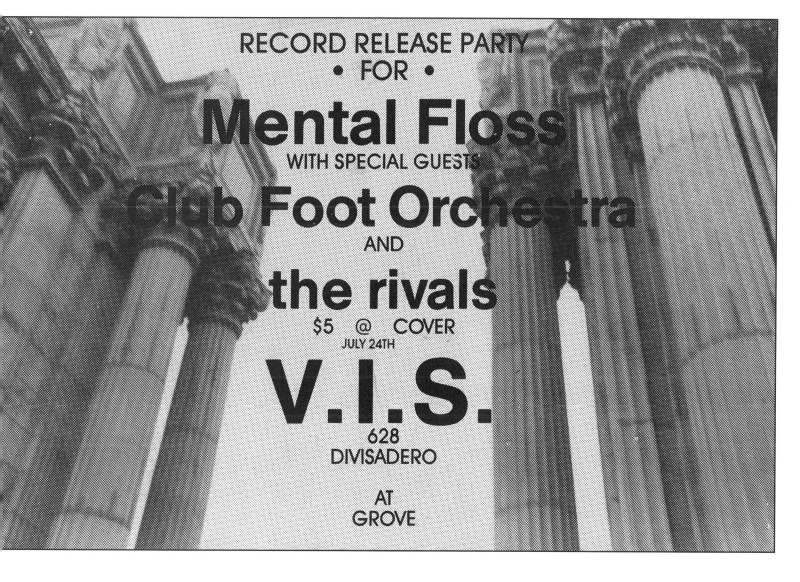

RECORD RELEASE PARTY
• FOR •

Mental Floss
WITH SPECIAL GUESTS

Club Foot Orchestra
AND

the rivals
$5 @ COVER
JULY 24TH

V.I.S.
628
DIVISADERO

AT
GROVE

THE BRIDGE

WITH THE BUSBOYS

Tickets!!
d-i-A-l
468-1870
Anytime

At the Stone S.F   AUG. 10, 1985   STARTS AT 8:00 P.M

ROY LONEY and the PHANTOM MOVERS

Cover: $2
September 15th

Video: Ted Ledru & Co
Disks: Arne Brogger

at the
I-BEAM   1748 Haight (at Cole) ● 9:30-2:00 am

Photo: Jack Dart

S.M.E.G.M.A.

DAY AT THE FARM II

7 SECONDS · FANG
TOKEN ENTRY
VICTIM'S FAMILY
THE MIGHTY FARM BAND

SUN. JULY 27   4 P.M. $7.00   1499 POTRERO

SUB HUM ANS
UK

SCREAM
NY

worlds apart
tour USAT 5

WHERE → THE FARM
WHEN → Fri. May 24th
HOW MUCH → 431-1326

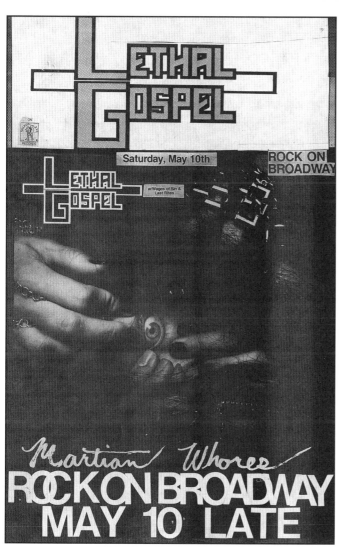

LETHAL GOSPEL

Saturday, May 10th

ROCK ON BROADWAY

LETHAL GOSPEL

w/Wages of Sin & Last Rites

Martian Whores

ROCK ON BROADWAY
MAY 10 LATE

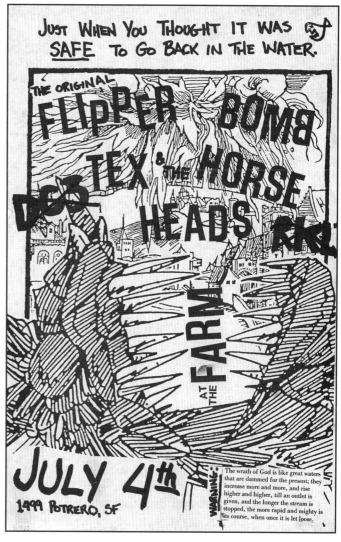

JUST WHEN YOU THOUGHT IT WAS SAFE TO GO BACK IN THE WATER.

THE ORIGINAL
FLIPPER   BOMB
TEX & THE HORSE
DC3   HEADS   RKL

AT THE FARM

JULY 4th
1499 POTRERO, SF

WARNING: The wrath of God is like great waters that are dammed for the present; they increase more and more, and rise higher and higher, till an outlet is given, and the longer the stream is stopped, the more rapid and mighty is its course, when once it is let loose.

KOMMUNITY FK
FRIDAY MAY 2, 1986

THE FARM
1499 POTRERO

SURROGATE TELEVISION FOR THE BRAIN-DEAD
FEATURING
TRIAL
BLACK ATHLETES
MOD MACH

FRIDAY OCT. 11, 1985 9PM $5
THE FARM 1499 POTRERO SF

TYPHOON
RECORD RELEASE PARTY
BOMB

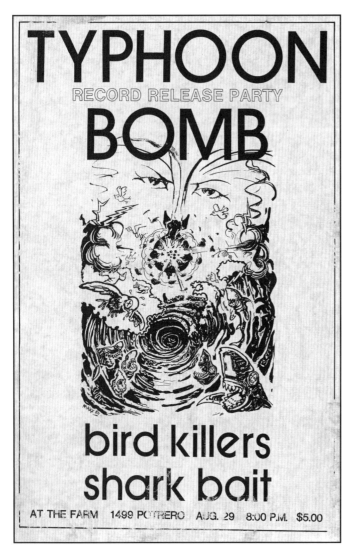

bird killers
shark bait

AT THE FARM   1499 POTRERO   AUG. 29   8:00 P.M. $5.00

Wiring Dept. Magazine Benefit
Sunday, October 12
FLAMING LIPS
RHYTHM and NOISE
GLORIOUS DIN
RAINING HOUSE
PLATEAU ENSEMBLE
WEDNESDAY MORNING,
3 A.M.

ALL AGES WELCOME
$5 — From 7 to 12:30

THE FARM 1499 POTRERO

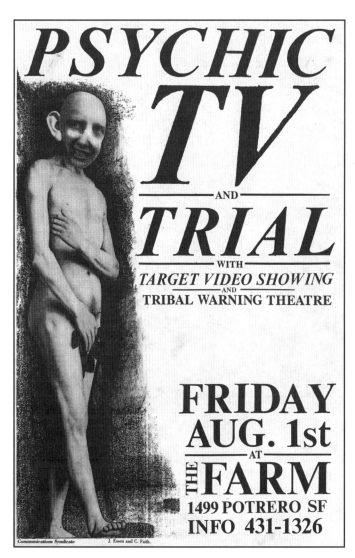

PSYCHIC
TV
AND
TRIAL
WITH
TARGET VIDEO SHOWING
AND
TRIBAL WARNING THEATRE

FRIDAY
AUG. 1st
AT
THE FARM
1499 POTRERO SF
INFO 431-1326

Communications Syndicate   J. Essen and C. Faith.

NEW LIFE

AT THE FARM
1499 Potrero ave.

BENEFIT FOR:
The Bayview industrial
Burn Victems.

Sunday 3:30 p.m.
MAY 18

FRIGHT WIG
AFLICTED
Psychic ORPHANS
CELEBRITY SKIN

AND SPECIAL GUESTS!!!
BABY Jesus
AND THE HOUSE COAT
Contingents

N BVCK AND THE BAREBOTTOM BOYS

+ POETS
SPEAKERS
AND
Guitar Solos!!!

"IS IT A BOY-OR IS IT A GIRL?"

VISIONS OF DEATH
SEPTIC
ROCK ON BROADWAY
WITH
SCHIZO AND
CRUSADER
HEADLINING

Sybil

SPECIMEN
ON BROADWAY   435 BROADWAY
San Francisco

NOV. 2 ND.

BARBARIC CABARET ACTS!....

TACKY TO THE MAX!!

HEAVY METAL MANIA
HEAVY BENEFIT FOR #16
with BLIND ILLUSION
ON BROADWAY
NOVEMBER Friday 22nd 7PM
BE THERE EARLY & STAY LATE
BLIND ILLUSION
and... HEATHEN CONTROL
WARNING
Squirt's Revenge
BANG!
PLUS SPECIAL GUESTS!
FREE METAL MANIAS
Deathsquad victims are often disfigured beyond recognition
Photo by Ron Kinney
THE REBEL NOV. 22, 1985
Metal Mania
ALL AGES ALLOWED NO I.D. REQUIRED!!!
SHOW STARTS EARLY BANDS GO ON AT 7PM
HEAVY METAL HEADBANGERS
LISTEN TO THEM! IT'LL BE HARD TO HEAR ANYTHING ELSE!!!
Metal Mania

SEARCH & DESTROY PRODUCTIONS PRESENTS
'LOUDER FASTER SHORTER'
FILM BY MINDAUGIS
W/ UXA DILS AVENGERS SLEEPERS MUTANTS
HALF BROKE M.C. DETROIT
Outlaws
MABUHAY Gardens
443 Broadway · San Francisco
956-3315
APPEARING LIVE:
A DIRKSEN-MILLER PRODUCTION
MUTANTS
UXA
SLEEPERS
SAT. NOV. 17 11PM
TICKETS 4.50 AVAILABLE AT MABUHAY & BASS TICKET OUTLETS

DAMON'Z
19th NOV. 16th 9PM NOTE
16 S.F.
20th NOV. MAB 9PM

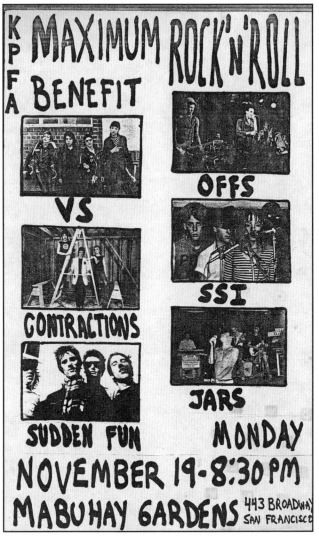

KPFA MAXIMUM ROCK'N'ROLL BENEFIT
VS
OFFS
CONTRACTIONS
SSI
JARS
SUDDEN FUN
MONDAY
NOVEMBER 19 - 8:30 PM
MABUHAY GARDENS
443 BROADWAY SAN FRANCISCO

Mister Hyde

DIE YOUNG STAY PRETTY

AT THE ROCK ON BROADWAY   SAT. JAN. 9TH

LIVE   SUN. NOV. 22

FROM RENO Nv.

Action FIGURE

WITH TOXIC REASONS

PLUS BEATNIGS

NO USE FOR A NAME

AND J.C. HOPKINS

GILMAN ST. AT WHAREHOUSE   Berkely Ca.

KENNEL CLUB
628 DIVISADERO

s 12/20	**CAPITOL RECORDS HOLIDAY PARTY** *free records free promo*
t 12/22 K.U.S.F. RECKLESS RECORDS CALANDER MAGAZINE TRASH!	**THE SISTERS OF MERCY**
w 12/23	**CALENDAR MAGAZINE ANNUAL XMAS BASH**
t 12/24	**JANE GENET PLATINUM XMAS PARTY**
f 12/25	closed. merry christmas
s 12/26	**MR. DOG BEATNICK BEACH**

NEW YEAR'S EVE BASH

fishbone

BASS TICKETMASTER.   RING IN THE NEW YEAR

NIGHTBREAK

HARD RAIN

SILVER THREADS

SAT 25 JUNE

SPEEDWAY RECORDS

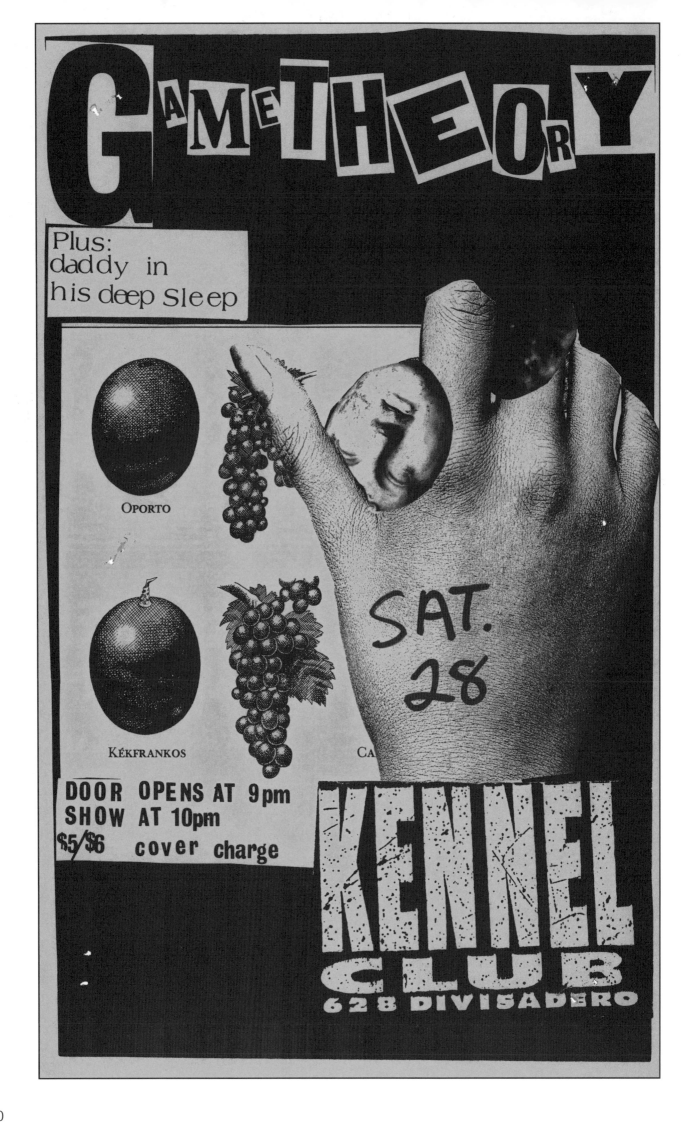

50

51

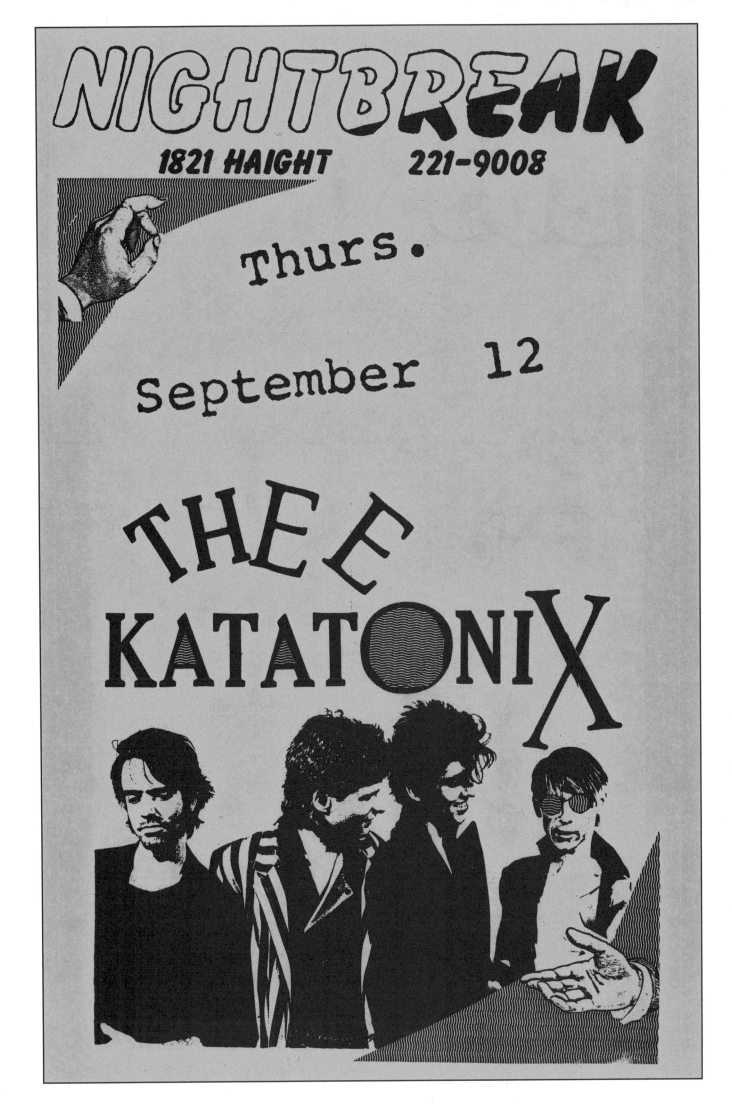

NIGHTBREAK

1821 HAIGHT   221-9008

Thurs.

September 12

THEE KATATONIX

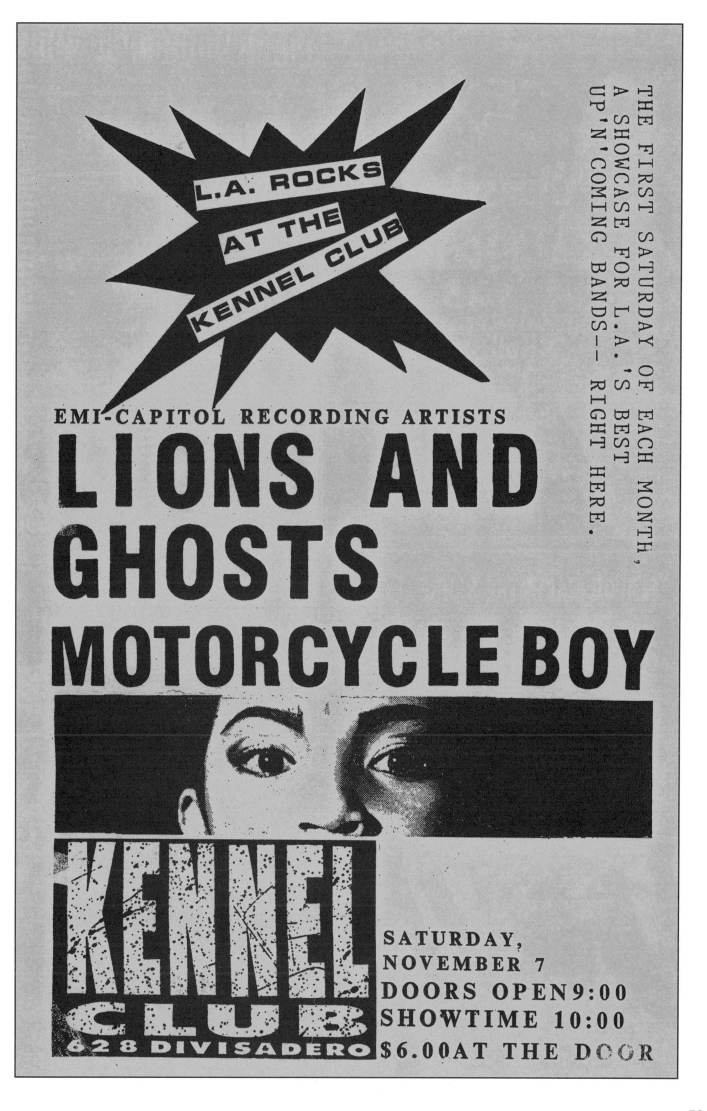

L.A. ROCKS AT THE KENNEL CLUB

THE FIRST SATURDAY OF EACH MONTH, A SHOWCASE FOR L.A.'S BEST UP'N'COMING BANDS— RIGHT HERE.

EMI-CAPITOL RECORDING ARTISTS

LIONS AND GHOSTS
MOTORCYCLE BOY

KENNEL CLUB
628 DIVISADERO

SATURDAY, NOVEMBER 7
DOORS OPEN 9:00
SHOWTIME 10:00
$6.00 AT THE DOOR

TEX &
the
Horseheads
FRIDAY
9/23
with
Hollyrock
at
Chatterbox
$4.00 10:30
21 & OVER
It's drinkin' time!

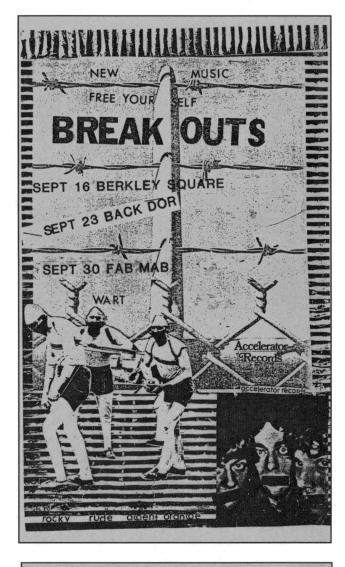

NEW   MUSIC
FREE YOUR SELF
BREAK OUTS
SEPT 16 BERKLEY SQUARE
SEPT 23 BACK DOR
SEPT 30 FAB MAB
WART
Accelerator Records
accelerator records
rocky rude agent orange

FLAVOR MAKES THE SAUCE
Thee Hellhounds
THE LEGENDARY STARDUST COWBOY
TEXORCIST
THE WANNA BE TEXANS

CHECK ONE	CHECK ONE
☐ PISTOL	☐ Revolver
	☐ Semi-automatic
	☐ Bolt Action
☐ RIFLE	☐ Lever Action
	☐ Pump
☐ SHOTGUN	☐ Single Shot
	☐ Obl. Barrel

SATURDAY OCTOBER 24
at the Kennel Club
628 DIVISADERO
931-1914

DEATHRANCH

Music: MODMACH
Visuals: EASE MEDIA and ODDERNMART
Guests: DEATH RANCH
Admission: THREE DOLLARS

at: BANNAM PLACE   50a Bannam Alley
Saturday, August 24 8pm to10pm

NIGHTBREAK
FRIDAY 8 JAN
PRAY FOR RAIN

SHOW STARTS AT 10:30 TIX 5$ at the door
also appearing:

CAPTURE THE FLAG

WIRETRAIN
with
The Mysteries

WEDNESDAY
MARCH 30

KENKEL CLUB
628 DIVISADERO
SAN FRANCISCO

$6.00 at the door
Doors open at 9pm
Showtime: 10pm

Tickets available at BASS

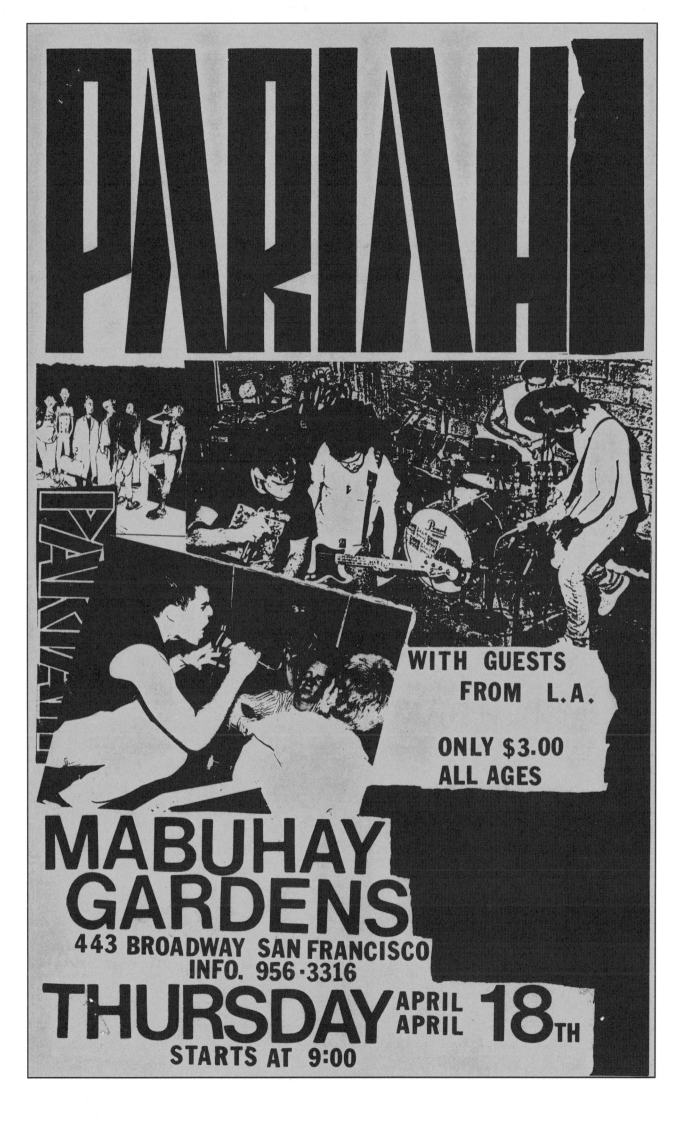

PARIAH

WITH GUESTS
FROM L.A.

ONLY $3.00
ALL AGES

MABUHAY
GARDENS
443 BROADWAY SAN FRANCISCO
INFO. 956-3316
THURSDAY APRIL 18TH
APRIL
STARTS AT 9:00

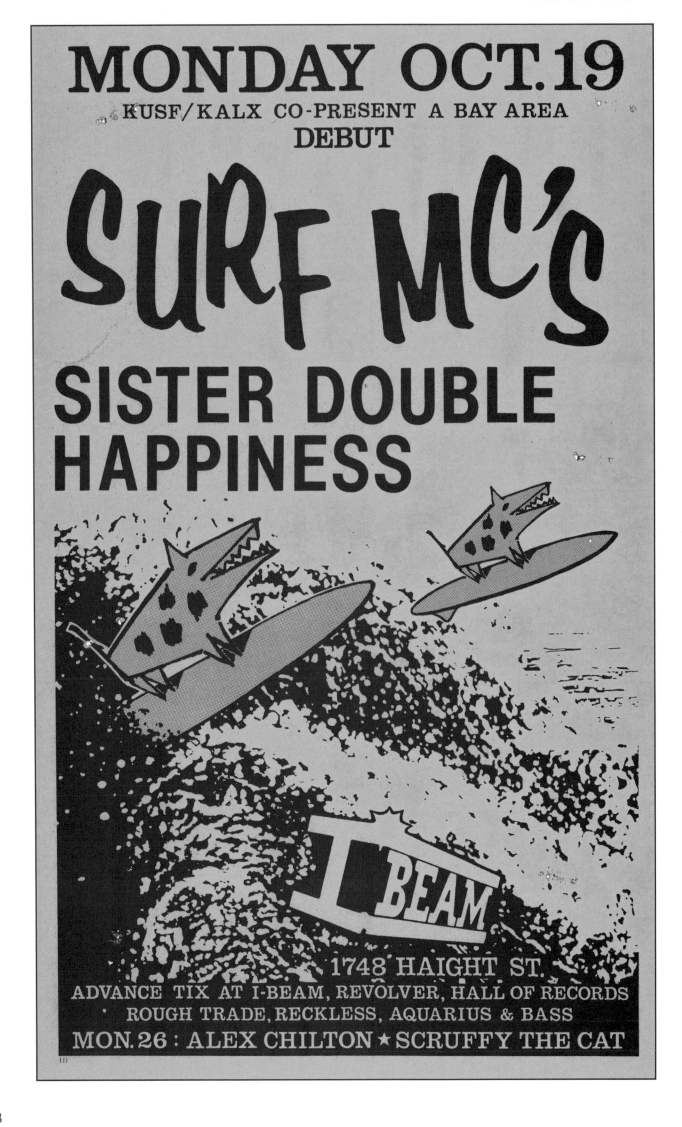

NIGHTBREAK
sea hags
Thurs Jan 2?
ALTAR DE FEY

221 9008

1821 Haight St.

EVERY SUNDAY 3–9pm

LIVE BANDS

serving fresh sushi hot sake

NO COVER DJ
this sunday

M-1 ALTERNATIVE   DEAN STREET

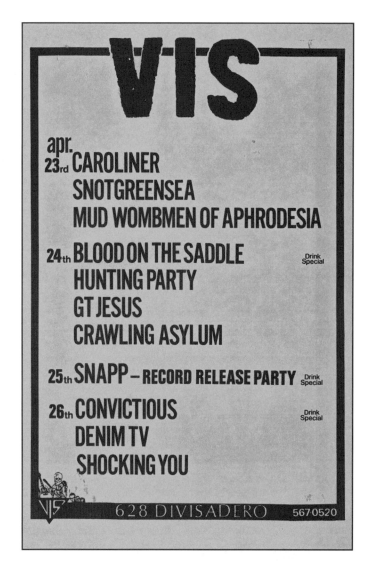

VIS

apr.
23rd CAROLINER
SNOTGREENSEA
MUD WOMBMEN OF APHRODESIA

24th BLOOD ON THE SADDLE   Drink Special
HUNTING PARTY
GT JESUS
CRAWLING ASYLUM

25th SNAPP – RECORD RELEASE PARTY   Drink Special

26th CONVICTIOUS   Drink Special
DENIM TV
SHOCKING YOU

628 DIVISADERO   567 0520

Zero

JOHN FAREY   STEVE KIMOCK   STEVE WOLF   GREG ANTON   JOHN CIPOLLINA
PO Box 299   WHIRLED RECORDS   415-663-1695
Lagunitas, CA 94938   415-459-3850

with
THE GREGG ALLMAN BAND

SAT. MAY 11 8 P.M. STONE S.F.
SUN. MAY 12 9 P.M. KEYSTONE Palo Alto

with
JAMES BLOOD ULMER
THURS. MAY 16 9 P.M. COTATI CABARET

MISSILE HARMONY with LAWN VULTURES
F. Jan.1 11 PM

NIGHTBreak
1821 Haight St

59

IMPULSE F

at
VIS CLUB
628 DIVISADERO
DOORS OPEN 9:00
FRI. NOVEMBER 22
$5

WITH
CRAWL AWAY
MACHINE

FRIDAY JUNE 26
BOSS HOSS

CHATTERBOX
853 VALENCIA

NIGHTBREAK
SPANISH
ELVIS

FRI
APR
8

SPEEDWAY
RECORDS

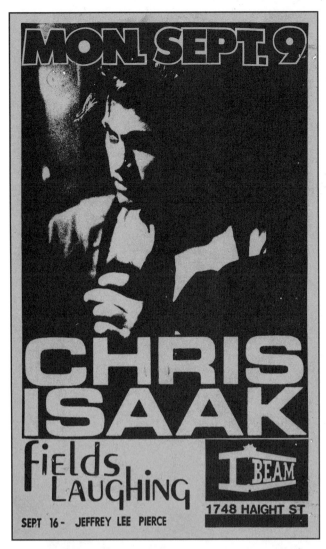

MON. SEPT. 9

CHRIS ISAAK

fields Laughing

I BEAM
1748 HAIGHT ST.

SEPT 16 - JEFFREY LEE PIERCE

SATURDAY
APRIL 23
DAVID LINDLEY
El Rayo-X

Doors open 9pm
Showtime: 10pm
$14 at the door
$13 at BASS

For Pep   For Fun
For "Enjoymint"

KENNEL CLUB
628 DIVISADERO

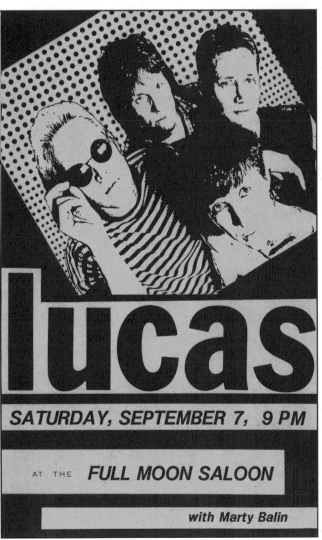

lucas

SATURDAY, SEPTEMBER 7, 9 PM

AT THE FULL MOON SALOON

with Marty Balin

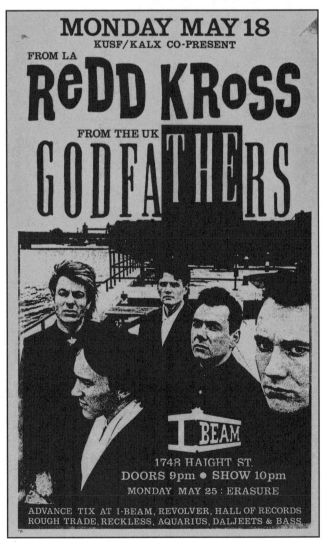

MONDAY MAY 18
KUSF/KALX CO-PRESENT
FROM LA
ReDD KRoSS
FROM THE UK
GODFATHERS

I BEAM
1748 HAIGHT ST.
DOORS 9pm • SHOW 10pm
MONDAY MAY 25 : ERASURE

ADVANCE TIX AT I-BEAM, REVOLVER, HALL OF RECORDS
ROUGH TRADE, RECKLESS, AQUARIUS, DALJEETS & BASS

64

Clear & Distinct Ideas & GOLDENVOICE Presents
FROM ENGLAND

G.B.H.
Metal Church
Verbal Abuse   Corosion of Conformity

FRIDAY, JUNE 14

THE FARM
7:30 PM   1499 POTRERO

ADVANCE TICKETS TICKETRON
INFORMATION: 431-1326

Michael Hall 85

MY SIN
domino theory
FULL MOON SALOON
9 PM WED. SEPT. 11   1725 HAIGHT

MONDAY AUGUST 17
KUSF/KALX CO-PRESENT A SF EXCLUSIVE

I-BEAM
1748 HAIGHT

NEW MODEL ARMY

POISON 13

ADVANCE TIX AT I-BEAM, REVOLVER, HALL OF RECORDS
ROUGH TRADE, RECKLESS, AQUARIUS & BASS
MONDAY AUGUST 24: CHRIS & COSEY • SPK

THE REPLACEMENTS
FLYING COLOR
THE CATHEADS
TEN TALL MEN

SAT. MAY 3RD 9PM
THE FILLMORE
1805 GEARY

NIGHTBREAK

NETTWERK PRODUCTIONS

MANUFACTURE

FROM BOSTON, WHERE ELSE?

12" AND VIDEO *ARMED FORCES* AVAILABLE ON NETTWERK RECORDS
VIDEOS: TACKHEAD · RENEGADE · NITZER EBB · SOUND WAVE · FRONT 242 **DEBUT S.F. SHOW!**

N S+M PRODUCTIONS **THURSDAY MARCH 3**

SALEM 66
only Bay Area appearance!

plus
Shiva Dancing

KALX -   KFJC -   KUSF

Thurs. Dec. 12

628 Divisidero **VIS Club** at Grove

KUSF PRESENTS

WITNESSES

BOSS HOSS
MESS TENT

V.I.S.

628 DIVISADERO
TUESDAY, JULY 30
9:00 P.M.

CRUSADER

OCTOBER ROCKS ON BROADWAY !:

BRANNON

Thursday 17th
the
STONE
10 PM

Thursday 24th
the
Chi Chi
11 PM

&

THE
boys

Thursday 31st Halloween Night
AT THE
STONE
10 PM

opening for

GREG KIHN

in association with **KMEL**
tickets available at BASS

THE RAZERS

NON FICTION
PANDEMANIA

AT
THE
V.I.S.
628 DIVISADERO

SAT.
APRIL 19
10:00

Faith No More   Glorious Din
23 Screams   Electric Piece
SATURDAY JULY 20
V.I.S. 628 Divisadero

THE RAZERS

**WED.
MARCH 4
9 pm**

75 cent beer!

VIS CLUB 628 DIVISADERO

PENELOPE HOUSTON

with

The LoNGSHoREMEn

Ivy NiCholsoN
Riches to Rags to Rock!

at the
STONE
8:PM
18 and over

DEBoRA IYaLL

MARCH 9 WED

MONDAY
SEPT. 28

KUSF/KALX
CO-PRESENT

FAITH NO MORE

THE SEAHAGS

1748 HAIGHT ST.

I BEAM

MONDAY OCTOBER 5 : ZAPP

+CRYPTOVISION RECORDS [new york] PRESENT:

THE MOD FUN

APPEARING LIVE at:
The MAB
This SUNDAY, APRIL 27-10PM
Only S.F. SHOW!

cryptovision

NEW LP "dorothy's dream" OUT NOW! on—
CRYPTOVISION, PO BOX 1812 N.Y. N.Y. 10009   DISTRIBUTED BY—DUTCH EAST, SYSTEMATIC, MIDNITE

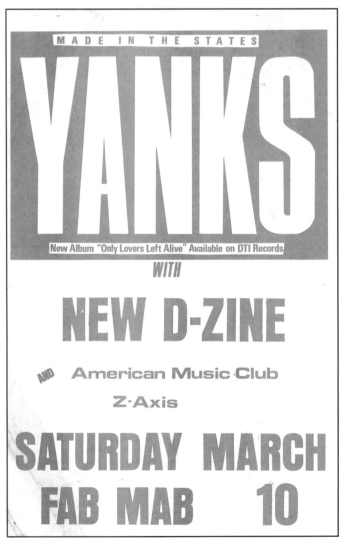

MADE IN THE STATES

YANKS

New Album "Only Lovers Left Alive" Available on DTI Records

WITH

NEW D-ZINE

AND American Music·Club

Z·Axis

SATURDAY MARCH 10
FAB MAB

4th MGAABRUDHEANSthYS

Palmetto State
Smear
Psuedonym

THE DEATH OF OPERA
BY JOHN GUNNISON-WISEMAN

and

LAW
COMED

WASTED YOUTH
BLAST
PIT

JULY 12th
ROCK
ON
BROAD-WAY
S.F.
$7.00
Starts
6 P.M
NO
N.G.S

LIES?

SUBJECT TO CHANGE

AT: The Sound of Music
Sat, Apr 4 162 Turk (A BAND)
NEW!! IMPROVED!!! sounds like

Mon.
April 6
AT: The
Mabuhay

KING CRIMSON
MAHAVISHNU
GANDHI + Good SEX!

Billy Wilder Tribute

the children's hour

NIGHTBREAK
SUN 10
5 pm
free
ON BROADWAY
WED 13
$5

(Sun mat 145)

Wed-Thur, Aug 27-28	DOUBLE	
	THE FORTUNE COOKIE	6:00, 10:00
Wed-Thur, Sept 3-4	THE APARTMENT	8:00
	KISS ME, STUPID	5:45, 10:00
Wed-Thur, Sept 10-11	THE FRONT PAGE	8:00
	ONE, TWO, THREE	6:00, 10:00
Wed-Thur, Sept 17-18	THE PRIVATE LIFE OF	
	SHERLOCK HOLMES	8:00
	LOST WEEKEND	6:00, 10:00

ROXIE CINEMA
3117 16th (at Valencia)   863-1087

The FARM

SOCIAL UNREST

SCREAMING SIRENS
from L.A.

SEA HAGS

POISON 13
from Austin Texas

the WEASELS

BARROOM PARTY

$5
8 PM
1499 POTERO AVE.

SAT. OCT. 12
S.F.
826-4290

READYMADES
and
TUXEDO MOON

FRI
FEB 17
11pm

with The BEANS

MABUHAY GARDENS

TELEPHONE:
(415) 956·3315
443 Broadway San Francisco
DIRKSEN-MILLER Production

70

LEILA
AND THE SNAKES

Premiering
Leila's New Work

PUNKULA

NO SISTERS
Plus Special Guests
Ed Mock, Doris Fish and Al-Fellahin

HALLOWEEN'78
Tues Oct 31 8:30pm

BIMBOS
Tickets at Bass

DESIGN: D EVENSON   PHOTO: EDDIE TROIA

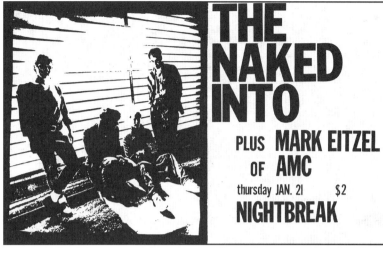

THE NAKED INTO

PLUS **MARK EITZEL**
OF **AMC**

thursday JAN. 21 $2
NIGHTBREAK

The Lords of Dark Metal...

Original Sin

Wednesday

Aug. 6, 1986

Starts at Six

at the Rock on Broadway

442 Broadway

Sin Francisco

Original Sin

with special guest

Vicious Fish

Original Sin

DIE KREUZEN *from Milwaukee* FRIGHTWIG *S.F.'s FINEST*
BULEMIA BANQUET *from L.A.* AND OTHER GUESTS
ALL AGES • EARLY SHOW • ALL AGES • ALL AGES • EARLY SHOW
MONDAY / MAR. 30
MAB $5

FALSE PROPHET
D.O.A. WE ARE BACK TO ROCK!
POSTER BY RANDY
tHE LASt DANCE
WATCHMEN
Sister Double Happiness
Jon t. 431-1326
THE LAST DANCE
SAT. OCT. 31st
NO mean NO
THE FARM 1499 Potrero
826-4290
WIN TICKETS ON KPOO 89.9 fm
wednesdays 3-6pm

WORLD'S CUTEST KILLERS'
Kathy Valentine formerly of the Go-Go's
&
Members of Girlschool,
PIL and Broken Homes
LIVE AT THE FENCING CENTER
April 25th *S.AT.*
Tickets $ 7.50 9 PM
40 N. 1st. S.J.

3¢ MAUS? GUITARS

HAUS? of WHEELS

SHORT DOGS GROW
SAT. OCT. TWELFTH
MAB ON BROADWAY

TYPHOON BOMB

8:00 P.M.
FRI. AUG. 29
1499 POTRERO
$5.00

8:00 P.M.
FRI. AUG. 29
1499 POTRERO
$5.00

RECORD RELEASE PARTY

SHARK BAIT
BIRD
KILLERS

AT THE FARM

Beer bellies

"Lock Up You're daughters"

ACID

MENTORS

Eat your hearts out

MAB - Nov. 8 - FRI.
Ruthies - Nov 9 - SAT

Carol Mohew

Saturday JANUARY 4, '86

Camper Van Beethoven
BLACK ATHLETES
Polkacide
STICK AGAINST STONE

THE FARM
for more information 826-4290
1499 Potrero
$5.00
Doors open 8:30

KUSF/KALX/KFJC CO-PRESENT A SF EXCLUSIVE
MONDAY JUNE 20
THROWING MUSES
PIXIES
I BEAM
1748 HAIGHT ST.
ADVANCE TIX AT I-BEAM, REVOLVER, HALL OF RECORDS
ROUGH TRADE, RECKLESS, AQUARIUS, SPEEDWAY & BASS
TR

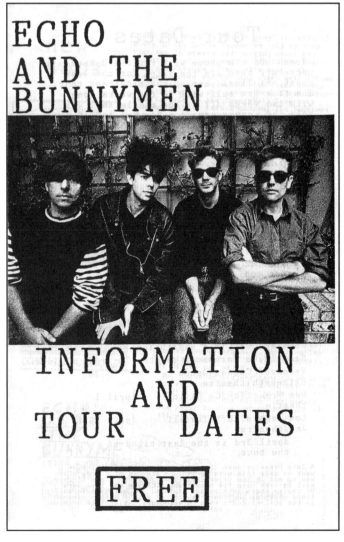

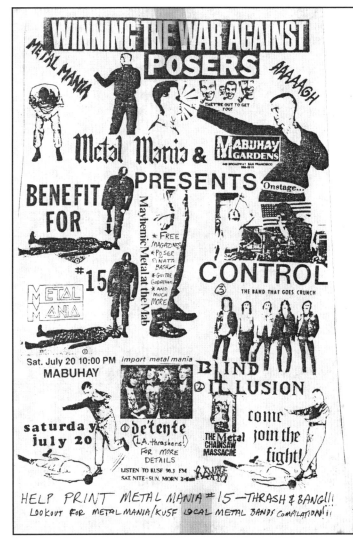

CAROLINER

RAINBOW FLESH DONATION for building a garbage farm

from the 1800's now teaching 1900's

Playing at midnight!

VOMIT Launch

popular Chico band!

one poisoned

one field ruled

not Sex Doll butt →

X = TAL

They are ready to ruin your religious thoughts. shiver!

WORLD OF POOH

with the fancy footworks

at the OASIS

THE HOLISTIC MEAT RACK

SEPT. 19th 1988 MON.

PRAY FOR RAIN

FRIDAY, MARCH 11

THE SEAHAGS

also BIRDKILLERS

SATURDAY MARCH 12

NIGHTBREAK

Photos Chris B...

THE ARRIVAL OF
EPISODE

A NEW **ORIGINAL PROGRESSIVE ROCK BAND** IN THE TRADITION OF YES, GENESIS & MOODY BLUES

DON'T MISS EPISODE IN CONCERT!

NEW GEORGE'S
4TH STREET · SAN RAFAEL
SUNDAY, OCT. 13

UNCLE CHARLIE'S
PARADISE DR · CORTE MADERA
SATURDAY, OCT. 19

CHI CHI CLUB
BROADWAY, SAN FRANSISCO
THURSDAY, NOV. 7

COMING TO THE CHI CHI DEC 13
GREAT Prog. Rock DOUBLE BILL
EPISODE & STARCASTLE

"FOURTUNES", a four-song cassette EP by EPISODE is now available.
For Tickets, Cassette and Fan Info: P.O. Box 12, Corte Madera CA, 94925. (415)381-1800

THURSDAY FEB. 11
FLYING COLOR
WATCHMEN
TERRAPLANE

FELINE FRIDAY

FRIDAY FEB. 12
CATHEADS
HARD RAIN
BALDO REX

SATURDAY FEB. 13
SPOT 1019
BUCK NAKED
& THE BAREBOTTOM BOYS
MCM & THE MONSTER
TERMINATORS OF
ENDEARMENT

SHOWTIME 10:00
$5.00 AT THE DOOR

SAN FRANCISCO MUSIC WORKS
WHY NOT?
2140 MARKET AT CHURCH

TYPHOON
RECORD RELEASE PARTY

SAFE SEX

WITH
HERU RAHA
and
BALDO REX

WARNING: BECUASE ASPECTS OF THIS PERFORMANCE MAY BE INTERPRETED BY SOME AS CONDONING BLACK MAGIC, MURDER, SUICIDE, TORTURE, NECROPHILIA, AND ANTI-RELIGIOUS ACTS, WE ASK THAT PERSONS, WHO ARE EASILY OFFENDED OR INFLUENCED PLEASE NOT ATTEND.
--- THE MANAGEMENT

SAT APR 16 9pm $5
SF MUSICWORKS
2140 market

THURSDAY DEC. 10
WELCOME HOME SHOW
CATHEADS
HARRY'S PICKET FENCE
HALF BLIND

FRIDAY DEC. 11
AMERICAN MUSIC CLUB
AMERICAN ENGLISH
CAPTURE THE FLAG
30-20 RECOIL

SATURDAY DEC. 12
SEA HAGS
SHE-DEVILS
WHIPPING BOY
HERU RA HA

ALL SHOWS
$5.00 AT THE DOOR
OR $10.00 FOR ALL 3 SHOWS

WHY NOT?
SAN FRANCISCO MUSIC WORKS
2140 MARKET

82

RECORD BENEFIT

KUSF RNA

THUR. FEB 18

8 PM MUSIC $5.00 CHEAP

LOCAL ALL-STAR JAM
WITH KEVIN HUNTER of WIRE TRAIN
LESLIE MEDFORD of THE OPHELIA'S
ALSO MEMBERS of FLYING COLOR
THE CATHEADS · BLUE MOVIE
THE FURIES and THE McGUIRE'S
DENIM TV BEFORE THE JAM M-1 ALTERNATIVE

CLUB FOOT
orchestra

wild beasts

RECORD RELEASE
OASIS
11th & Folsom
TUESDAY MAY 20

AMERICAN ENGLISH
plus Housecoat Project
The Fillmore 4
and other surprises!

P. Simone

3RD ANNUAL UNDERGROUND
ART EXPO ▼ VERSUS ▼
2505 mariposa / york
SUNDAY MAY 22
2:00-8:00 PM $5

GLORIOUS DIN
STICK DOG
CAROLINER RAINBOW
WORLD OF POOH

MCS
455 10TH ST. AT HARRISON
8:30 SUN. DEC. 14

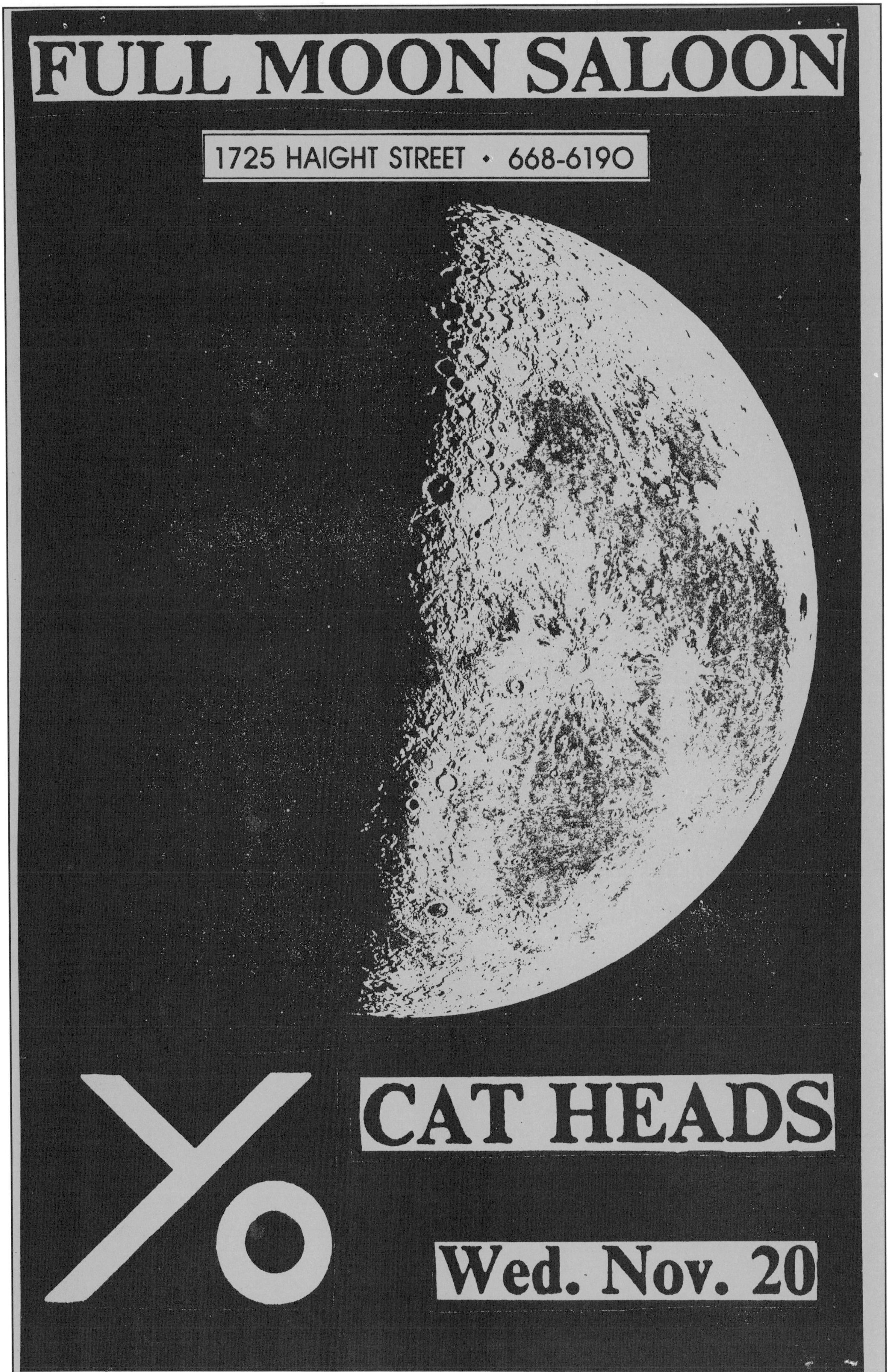
FULL MOON SALOON
1725 HAIGHT STREET • 668-6190
CAT HEADS
Wed. Nov. 20

NIGHTBREAK
Fri Nov 29
221-9008   1821 Haight St
Defectors
EVERY SUNDAY
LIVE BANDS
DJ 3pm-9pm
NO COVER
Serving: Hot Sake Fresh Sushi

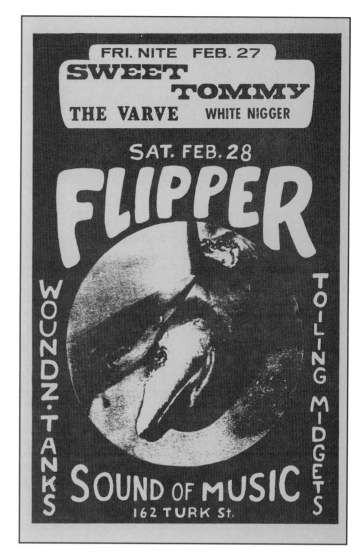

FRI. NITE FEB. 27
SWEET TOMMY
THE VARVE   WHITE NIGGER
SAT. FEB. 28
FLIPPER
WOUNDZ·TANKS   TOILING MIDGETS
SOUND OF MUSIC
162 TURK St.

ALL - FOOLS - RAP - EXTRAVAGANZA
FREAK - FEST - FRIDAY - APRIL - FIRST
Featuring
JOE MAMA
SURF MC'S
The Best in the West vs. NYC

RUN - DMC
LL COOL J
BEASTIE BOYS
MADONNAMAMA

FIREHOUSE 7
3160 16th Street, SF

APRIL
1st

Rx

ROCK
CORPORATION
PRESENT
Summer Fun
THE AVENGERS
THE PLUGZ
and
THE BRAINIACS
→ Sept. 1, 2 ←
14310 Oxnard Street ★ Van Nuys
(213) 997-9412

MOD MACH
(RECORD RELEASE)
V.I.S.
DEC. 6 (friday)

with POPART (L.A.)

Heavy Metal's Best!
KYLLERZ
& RENATA

World's Fastest Female Guitarist

SEPTEMBER 1 · 8PM

MABUHAY · 443 Broadway

SEPTEMBER 3 · 9PM

THE STONE · 412 Broadway

"EXPLODE WITH...

THE SNAPPERS

4TH of JULY!
THURSDAY NIGHT

ALSO:
· NANCY DE ROSS
AND · EXPOSE'

Chi Chi Theatre Club
Since 1964
440 Broadway, S.F.

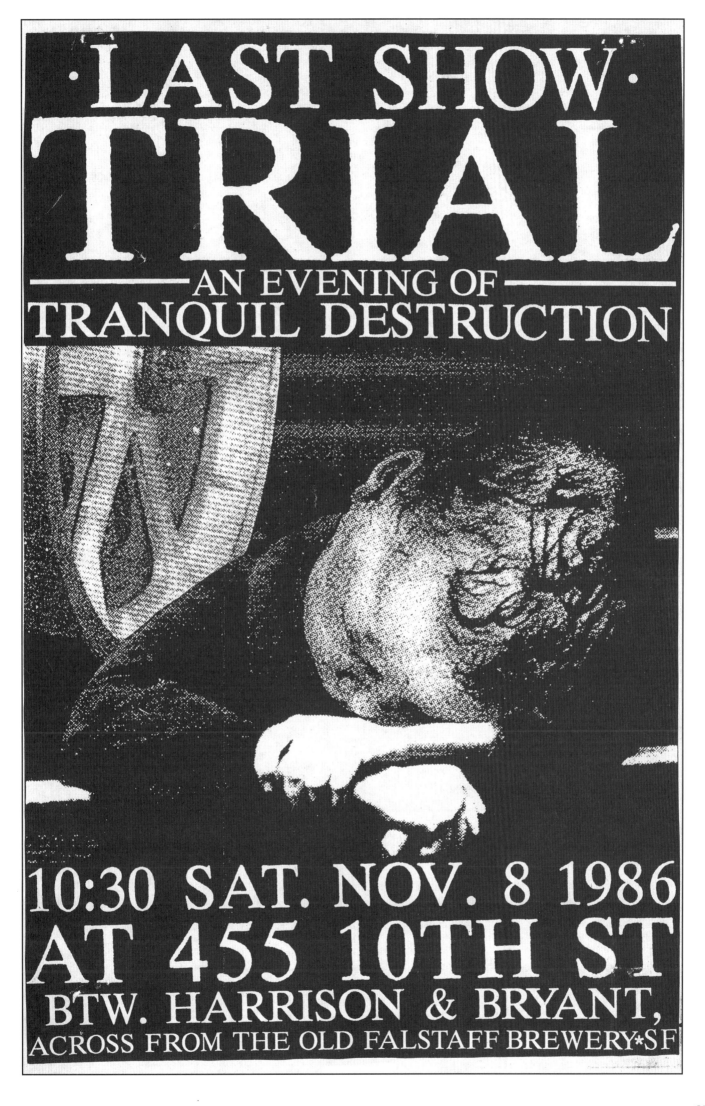

· LAST SHOW ·
TRIAL
AN EVENING OF
TRANQUIL DESTRUCTION

10:30 SAT. NOV. 8 1986
AT 455 10TH ST
BTW. HARRISON & BRYANT,
ACROSS FROM THE OLD FALSTAFF BREWERY*SF

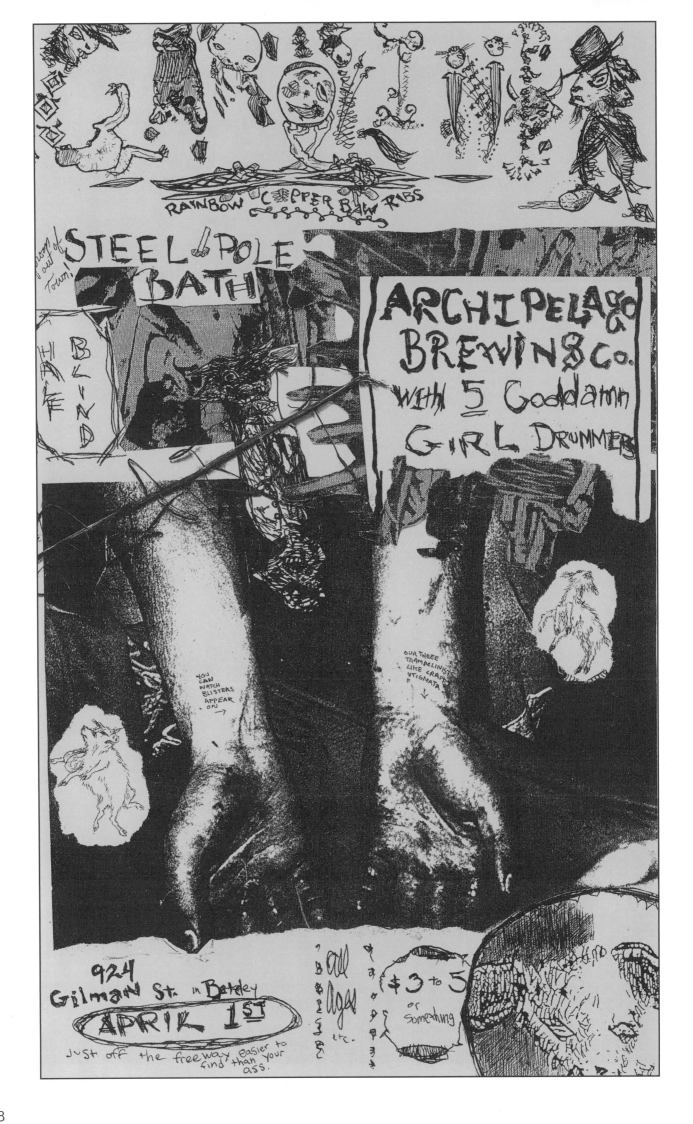

MONDAY JULY 27
KUSF/KALX CO-PRESENT
the Feelies
HUGO LARGO

I-BEAM
1748 HAIGHT ST.
ADVANCE TIX AT I-BEAM, REVOLVER, HALL OF RECORDS
ROUGH TRADE, RECKLESS, AQUARIUS & BASS
MONDAY AUGUST 3 : BIG BLACK ● THE WIPERS

·schools out at last bash·
TWO NIGHT'S ONLY WITH
JET BOY

wed june 18th
the stone
thur june 19th all ages
8 p.m.
keystone palo·alto

JET BOY   INFO: 9000 sunset blvd #405 LA, CA 90069

ALTERNATIVE TENTACLES RECORDS   NEW RELEASE   SHOW

NO MEANS NO
FROM CANADA
STICKDOG

VICTIM'S FAMILY
FRIDAY   APRIL 15
SAN FRANCISCO MUSIC WORKS
MARKET ST. AT CHURCH 9:30 P.M.

STICKDOG

SATURDAY   MARCH 5
SAN FRANCISCO MUSIC WORKS
MARKET ST. AT CHURCH 10:30 P.M.
ALSO APPEARING
BEATNIGS
SKINYARD

SPECIMEN

A NIGHTMARE ROMANCE
At The   Stone   RECORD RELEASE
412 BROADWAY 391-8282
THURSDAY CURFEW SHOW
June 5   6:00 PM to 10:00 PM
$6.50/7.50

NIGHTBREAK
FRIDAY, FEBRUARY 26
MISSLE
HARMONY
LIFE
PSYCLES
SATURDAY, FEBRUARY 27
HOUSE OF
WHEELS
SHIVA DANCING
SPEEDWAY RECORDS

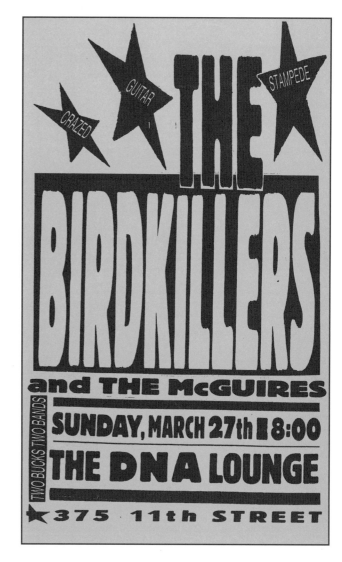

CRAZED GUITAR STAMPEDE
THE BIRDKILLERS
and THE McGUIRES
TWO BUCKS TWO BANDS
SUNDAY, MARCH 27th 8:00
THE DNA LOUNGE
375 11th STREET

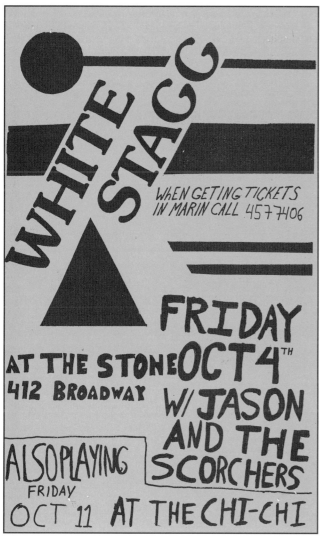

WHITE STAGG
WHEN GETING TICKETS IN MARIN CALL 457 7406
FRIDAY OCT 4th
AT THE STONE
412 BROADWAY
W/ JASON AND THE SCORCHERS
ALSO PLAYING FRIDAY
OCT 11 AT THE CHI-CHI

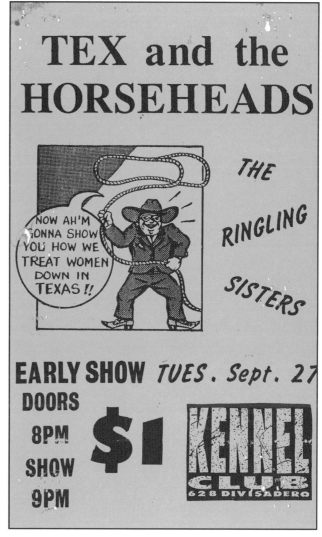

TEX and the HORSEHEADS
NOW AH'M GONNA SHOW YOU HOW WE TREAT WOMEN DOWN IN TEXAS!!
THE RINGLING SISTERS
EARLY SHOW TUES. Sept. 27
DOORS 8PM
SHOW 9PM
$1
KENNEL CLUB
628 DIVISADERO

SYSTEMS COLLAPSE & Shark Bait
Tues, Jan 26
at music works
2140 market

PIGLATIN
RECORD RELEASE PARTY
WITH
PENNSYLVANIA MAHONEY
& HER SAFE SEXTET

PLUS: PIG PINATAS, FOR THE PORCINE LUST IN ALL OF US
WEDNESDAY
APRIL 13
SHOWTIME 10:00
2140 MARKET AT CHURCH
NEW LP JACKPOT OUT NOW

SAN FRANCISCO MUSIC WORKS

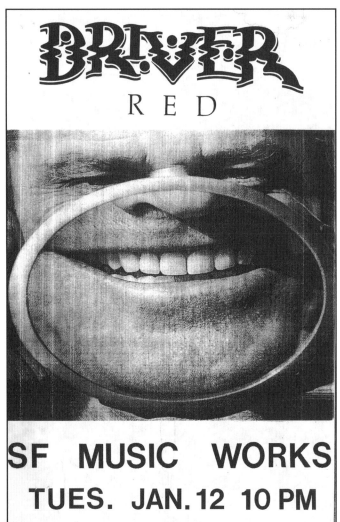

DRIVER
RED

SF MUSIC WORKS
TUES. JAN. 12 10 PM

BIG PHOBIC CHURCH

Death
Sex
Jesus
Meat

S.F. MUSIC WORKS 9 PM TUE. MARCH 22

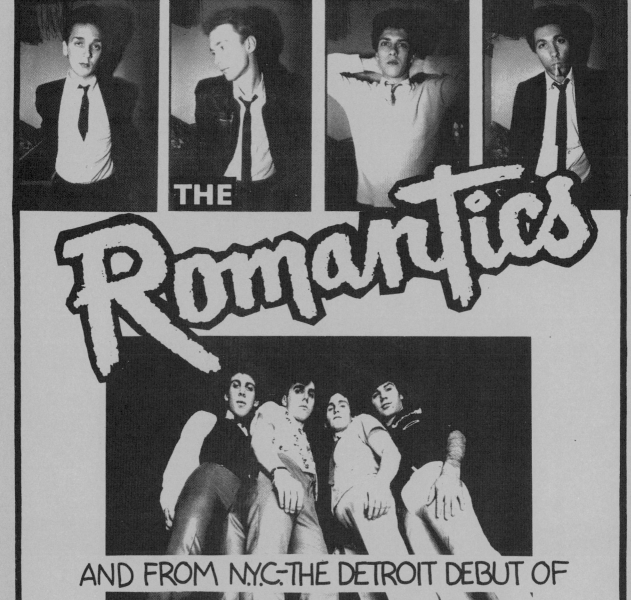

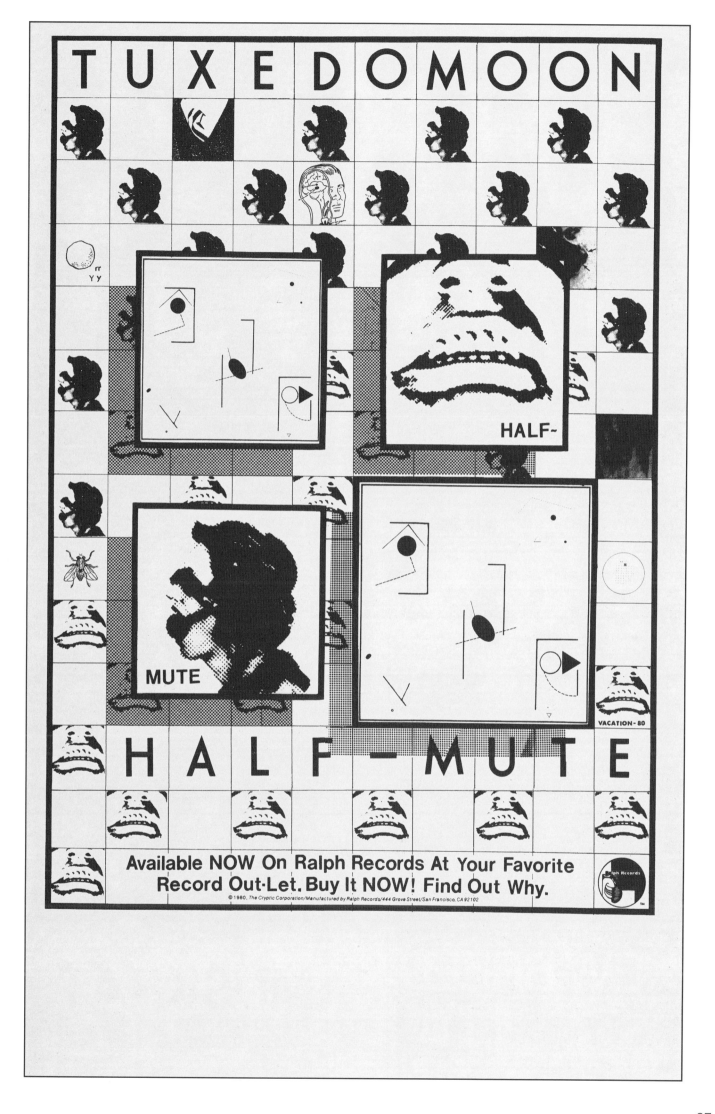

MON. SEPT. 23

KUSF/BAM/KALX CO-PRESENT

MINUTEMEN
SLOVENLY

SEPT 30 -
THE LUCY SHOW

OCT 7 - POISON GIRLS
BEAT RODEO

I BEAM
1748 HAIGHT ST

MON. JULY 21

KUSF/KALX CO-ANNOUNCE   BAY AREA EXCLU.

54·40
fIREHOSE

(EX-MINUTEMEN: MIKE & GEORGE, & ED FROM OHIO)

AUG. 4 - SCREAMING
BLUE MESSIAHS
CELIBATE RIFLES

AUG. 5 - THE CHURCH

I BEAM
1748 HAIGHT ST

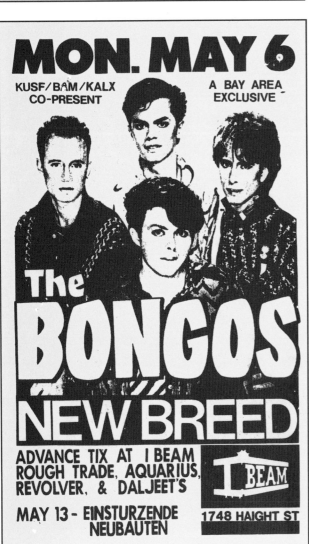

MON. MAY 6

KUSF/BAM/KALX CO-PRESENT   A BAY AREA EXCLUSIVE

The
BONGOS
NEW BREED

ADVANCE TIX AT I BEAM
ROUGH TRADE, AQUARIUS,
REVOLVER, & DALJEET'S

MAY 13 - EINSTURZENDE
NEUBAUTEN

I BEAM
1748 HAIGHT ST

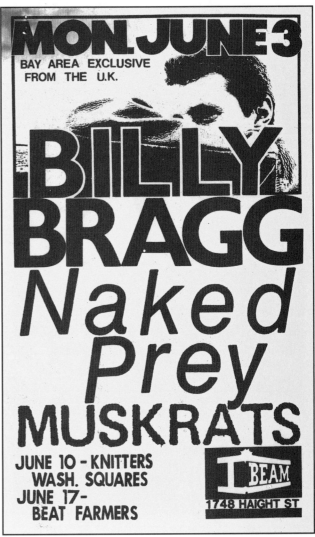

MON. JUNE 3

BAY AREA EXCLUSIVE FROM THE U.K.

BILLY BRAGG
Naked Prey
MUSKRATS

JUNE 10 - KNITTERS
WASH. SQUARES

JUNE 17 -
BEAT FARMERS

I BEAM
1748 HAIGHT ST

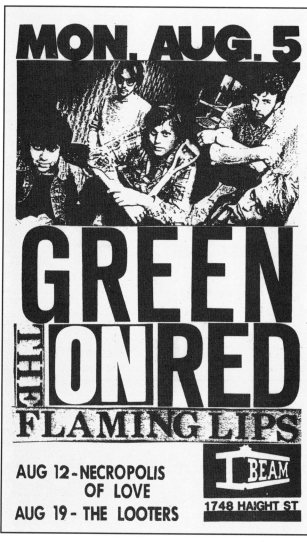

MON. AUG. 5

GREEN
THE ON RED
FLAMING LIPS

AUG 12 - NECROPOLIS
OF LOVE
AUG 19 - THE LOOTERS

I BEAM
1748 HAIGHT ST

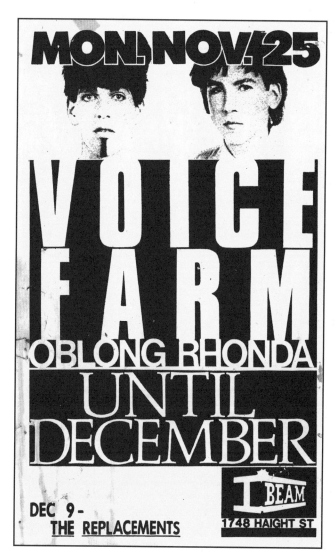

MON. NOV. 25

VOICE
FARM
OBLONG RHONDA
UNTIL
DECEMBER

DEC 9 -
THE REPLACEMENTS

I BEAM
1748 HAIGHT ST

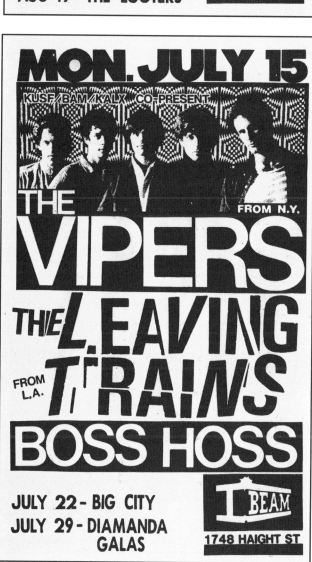

MON. JULY 15

KUSF/BAM/KALX CO-PRESENT

THE
VIPERS
FROM N.Y.
THE LEAVING
TRAINS
FROM L.A.
BOSS HOSS

JULY 22 - BIG CITY
JULY 29 - DIAMANDA
GALAS

I BEAM
1748 HAIGHT ST

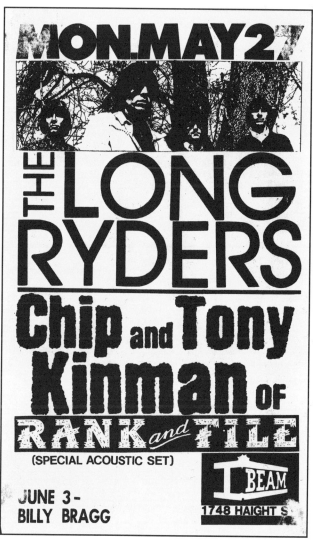

MON. MAY 27

THE LONG
RYDERS
Chip and Tony
Kinman OF
RANK and FILE
(SPECIAL ACOUSTIC SET)

JUNE 3 -
BILLY BRAGG

I BEAM
1748 HAIGHT S

KUSF/KALX CO-PRESENT A SF EXCLUSIVE
MONDAY MAY 4
THE MEKONS
CARMAIG de FOREST

I BEAM
1748 HAIGHT ST.
ADVANCE TIX AT I-BEAM, REVOLVER, HALL OF RECORDS
ROUGH TRADE, RECKLESS, AQUARIUS, DALJEETS & BASS
MONDAY MAY 11: THE LORRIES

MON. OCT. 14
KUSF/KALX CO-PRESENT A BAY AREA EXCLUSIVE
meat puppets
POISON 13
ADVANCE TIX AT I BEAM
ROUGH TRADE, AQUARIUS,
REVOLVER, & DALJEET'S
OCT 21-HOODOO GURUS
GENE LOVES JEZEBEL

I BEAM
1748 HAIGHT ST

MON. OCT. 28
KUSF/KALX CO-PRESENT FROM BOSTON
LYRES
YARD TRAUMA

NOV 4 -
BLUE RIDDIM

I BEAM
1748 HAIGHT ST

MON. APR. 22
BAY AREA EXCLUSIVE
THE VENTURES
"Walk Don't Run," "Hawaii Five-O"
FLYING COLOR
ADVANCE TIX AT I BEAM
ROUGH TRADE, AQUARIUS,
REVOLVER, & DALJEET'S

APR. 29- BONNIE HAYES
MAY 6- THE BONGOS

I BEAM
1748 HAIGHT ST

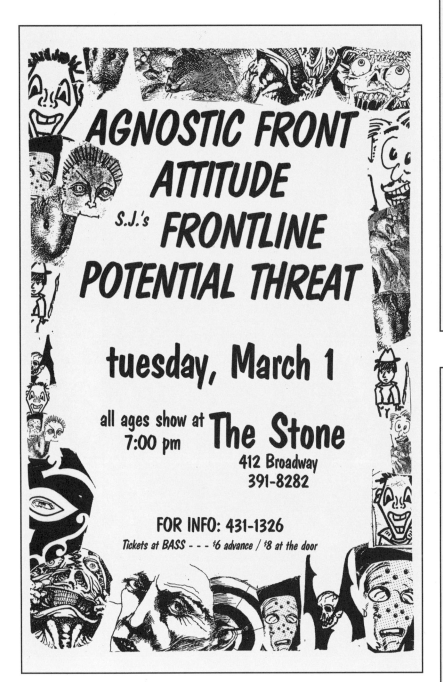

AGNOSTIC FRONT
ATTITUDE
S.J.'s FRONTLINE
POTENTIAL THREAT

tuesday, March 1

all ages show at **The Stone**
7:00 pm
412 Broadway
391-8282

FOR INFO: 431-1326
Tickets at BASS - - - $6 advance / $8 at the door

KALX, KUSF & THE KENNEL CLUB PRESENT

WACKY WEDNESDAY

this week:

DRUNK INJUNS

VIV AKAULDREN
(FROM DETROIT)   plus COUNT SPATULA

KENNEL CLUB
628 DIVISADERO

OCTOBER 14
10:30 sharp
$1.00 BEER ; popcorn

Independence through rock'n roll

4th of July   Golden Gate Park
Marx Meadows 1-5 PM

the
CONTRABAND

and   BOOTS
VKTMS
AMPUTATORS

Sound by C.A.E.

KSJO
92

Presented by
KSJO and
Faster/Louder Records

DJ DAVID BASSIN

PRIMUS
thurs may 22

NIGHTBREAK

APR 17 WAGES of SIN

THURS
NIGHTBREAK

221-9008
1821 HAIGHT

THE WHITE FRONTS

221-9008

MAY 15 THUR
DJ DAVID BASSIN
NIGHTBREAK

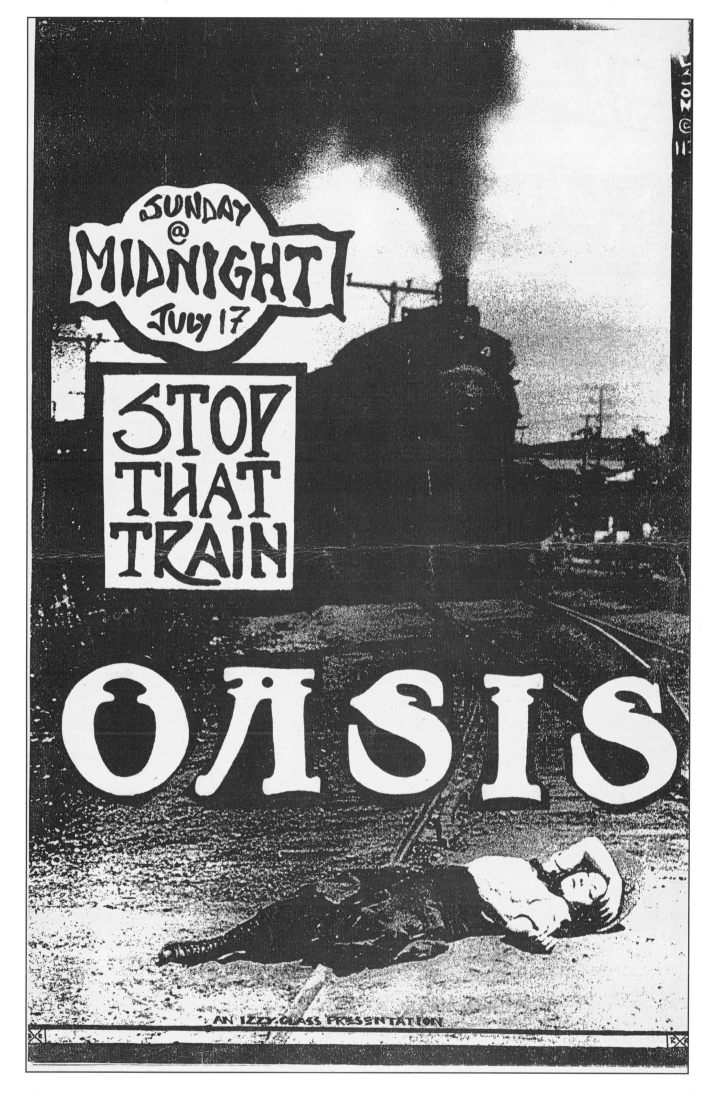

NIGHT BREAK

thrs aug 14

SCREAMING SIRENS

NIGHTBREAK

1821 HAIGHT   221-9008

GHOULS NIGHT OUT !! OCT 31

UNTIL DeCeMBeR

HALLOWEEN PARTY

THURSDAY

THE SEA HAGS

NIGHTBREAK

1821 HAIGHT   221-9008

Thurs Nov 21

LEGAL REINS

EVERY SUNDAY
LIVE BANDS
DJ 3pm - 9pm
NO COVER

Serving:
Hot Sake
Fresh Sushi

SEA HAGS

DJ JAMES WATKIns

NIGHT BREAK

FRI AU 29

NO GRENADES

MONDAY APRIL 6
KUSF/KALX CO-PRESENT
BUTTHOLE SURFERS
THE CELIBATE RIFLES

I-BEAM

ADVANCE TIX AT I-BEAM, REVOLVER, HALL OF RECORDS
ROUGH TRADE, RECKLESS, AQUARIUS, DALJEETS & BASS
MONDAY APRIL 13 : SKINNY PUPPY
MONDAY APRIL 20 : fIREHOSE ● SAQQARA DOGS

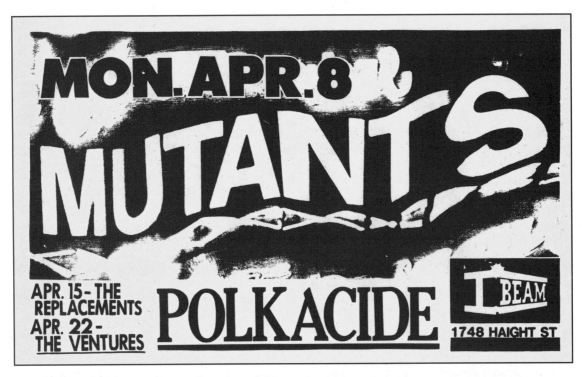

MON. APR. 8
MUTANTS
APR. 15 - THE REPLACEMENTS
APR. 22 - THE VENTURES
POLKACIDE
I BEAM
1748 HAIGHT ST.

Break a few hearts this Valentine's Day...
with US GIRLS!!

Thurs. Feb 13
9pm - 4am
Trocadero
4th & Bryant

Dance Contest:
salsa, funk, reggae

MON. DEC. 9
KUSF/KALX CO-PRESENT
THE REPLACEMENTS
THE PONTIAC BROTHERS
ADVANCE TIX AT I BEAM
ROUGH TRADE, AQUARIUS,
REVOLVER, & DALJEET'S
DEC 16 - FREAKY EXECUTIVES
DEC 23 - JESUS AND MARY CHAIN
FLAMING LIPS
I BEAM
1748 HAIGHT ST

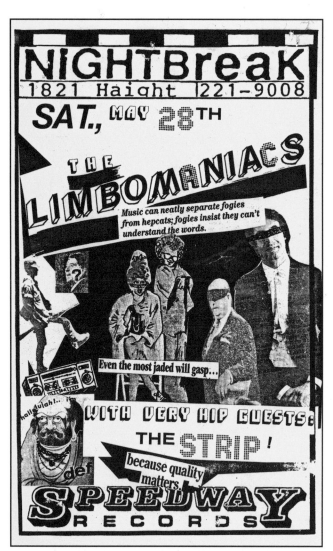

NIGHTBreak
1821 Haight 221-9008
SAT., MAY 28TH

THE LIMBOMANIACS

Music can neatly separate fogies from hepcats; fogies insist they can't understand the words.

Even the most jaded will gasp...

WITH VERY HIP GUESTS:
THE STRIP!

because quality matters

SPEEDWAY RECORDS

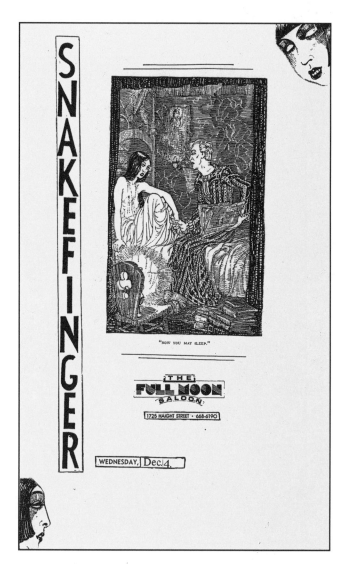

SNAKEFINGER

"NOW YOU MAY SLEEP."

THE FULL MOON SALOON
1725 HAIGHT STREET • 668-6190

WEDNESDAY, Dec. 14.

JETBOY

1 Year Anniversary Show
SAT JUNE 8th
AT THE ROCK ON BROADWAY
show starts at 9 jetboy on by 11
midnight til 2 jetboy party plus
lady jello wrestlers
jetboy info: send s.a.s.e. to P.O. box smoke sf.ca. 94159 0868
MODERN MANAGEMENT (415) 491-8303
COME SEE US JUNE 9th AT THE ROXY IN HOLLYWOOD W/ MADAM-X

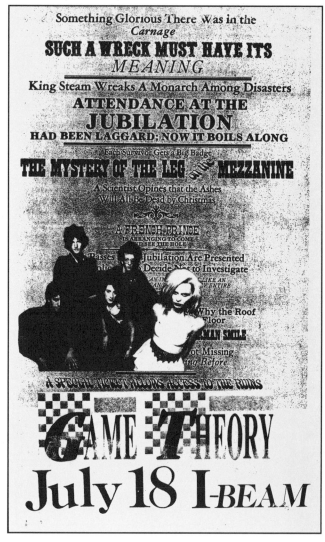

Something Glorious There Was in the *Carnage*
SUCH A WRECK MUST HAVE ITS MEANING
King Steam Wreaks A Monarch Among Disasters
ATTENDANCE AT THE JUBILATION
HAD BEEN LAGGARD; NOW IT BOILS ALONG
Each Survivor Gets a Big Badge
THE MYSTERY OF THE LEG UNDER MEZZANINE
A Scientist Opines that the Ashes
Will All Be Dead by Christmas
A FRENCH PRINCE
IS ARRANGING TO COME
D SEE THE HOLE

Passes   Jubilation Are Presented
                Decide Not to Investigate

Why the Roof

Not Missing
ing Before

A SPECIAL TICKET ALLOWS ACCESS TO THE RUINS

GAME THEORY
July 18 I-BEAM

110

FINAL WACKY WEDNESDAY AT THE KENNEL CLUB
FEATURING A BLOWOUT JAM AT MIDNIGHT

THE RINGLING SISTERS
FROM L.A.

FEATURING

PLEASANT of the SCREAMING SIRENS
TEXACALA of TEX & THE HORSEHEADS
JOHNETTE of CONCRETE BLONDE
DEBBIE of RASZEBRAE
DEBBIE of the DEVIL SQUARES
IRIS of the LAME FLAMES

PLUS FRITZ ALLSTARS

FEATURING EDDIE JENNINGS & members of
UNTIL DECEMBER SEAHAGS ANVIL CHORUS
BOHEMIAN LUV JONES LAWN VULTURES
BUCK NAKED & THE BAREBOTTOM BOYS
FLYING COLOR BUZZ IN THE SYSTEM

KENNEL CLUB
628 DIVISADERO

WED. FEB. 24
DOORS OPEN 8:00
SHOWTIME 9:00
$4.00 AT THE DOOR
TICKETS AVAILABLE AT BASS

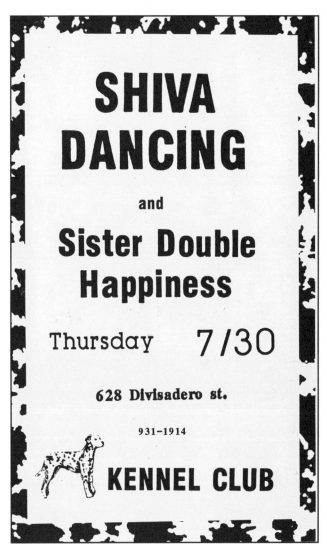

SHIVA DANCING

and

Sister Double Happiness

Thursday   7/30

628 Divisadero st.

931-1914

KENNEL CLUB

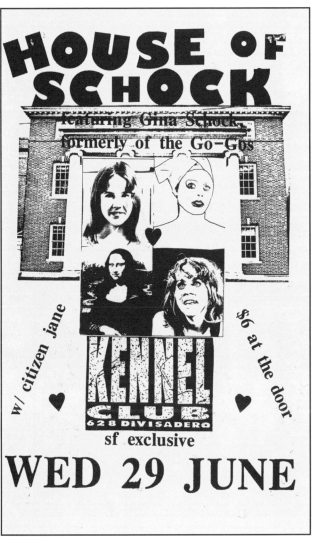

HOUSE OF SCHOCK
featuring Gina Schock,
formerly of the Go-Go's

w/ citizen jane

KENNEL CLUB
628 DIVISADERO

$6 at the door

sf exclusive

WED 29 JUNE

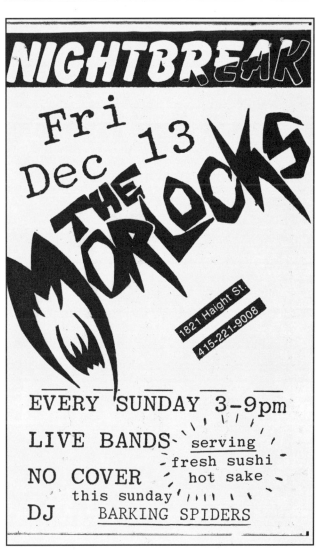

NIGHTBREAK

Fri Dec 13

THE MORLOCKS

1821 Haight St.
415-221-9008

EVERY SUNDAY 3-9pm

LIVE BANDS   serving
fresh sushi

NO COVER   hot sake
this sunday

DJ   BARKING SPIDERS

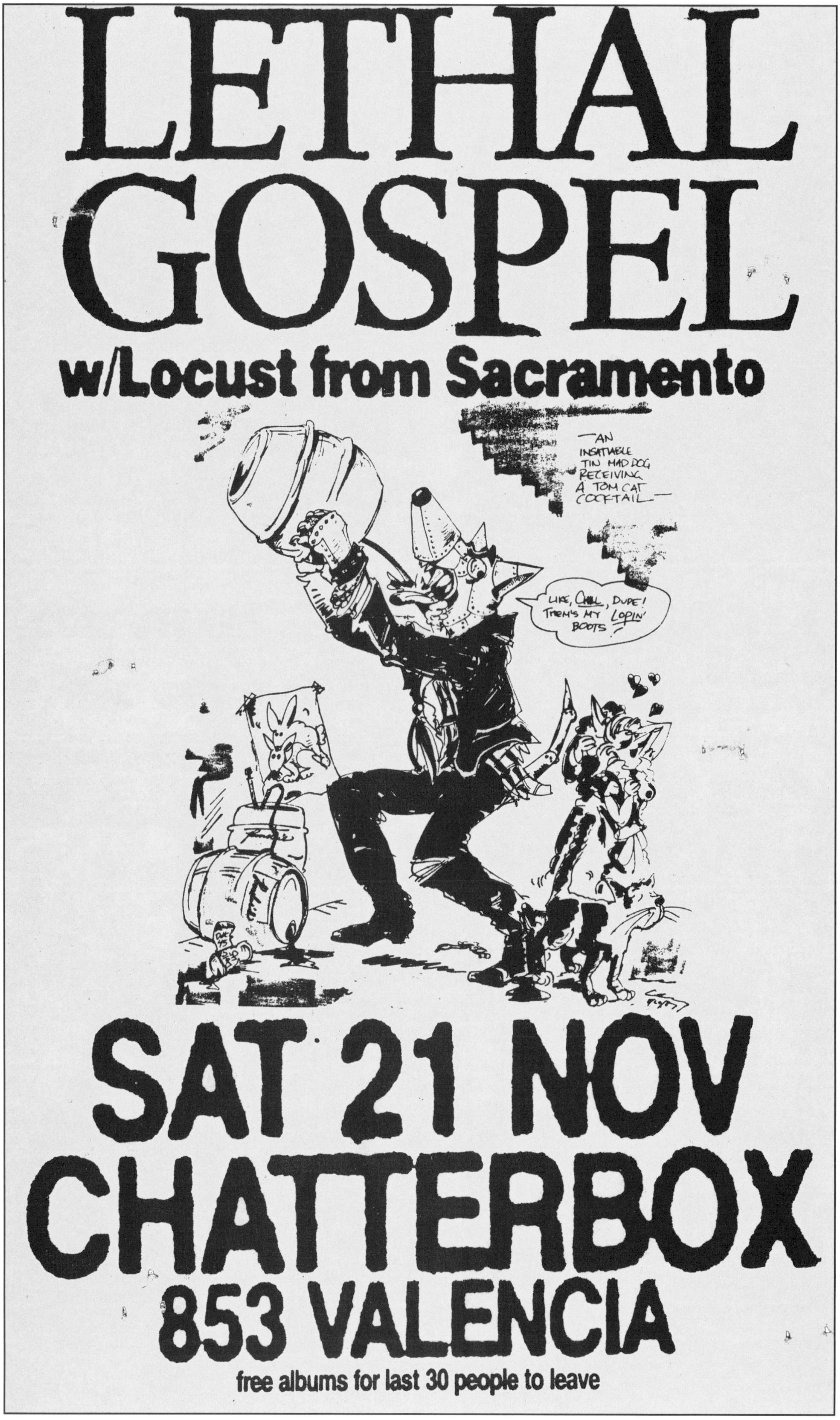
LETHAL GOSPEL
w/Locust from Sacramento
—AN INSATIABLE TIN MAD DOG RECEIVING A TOM CAT COCKTAIL—
LIKE, CHILL, DUDE! THEM'S MY LOPIN' BOOTS!
SAT 21 NOV
CHATTERBOX
853 VALENCIA
free albums for last 30 people to leave

A IS A
A IS A
A IS A
A IS A
A IS A.
A IS A.
A IS A

Are You Seeking Answers?

The Chi-Chi Club
440 Broadway
SAN FRANCISCO

AUG. 28
10:00 p.m.

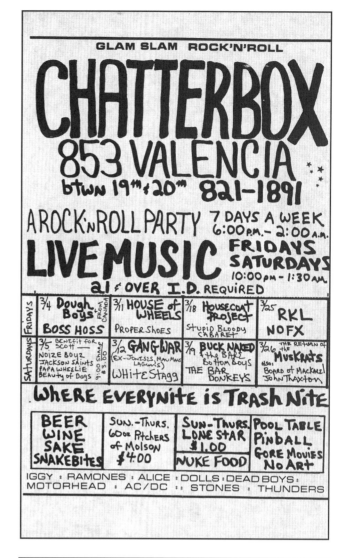

GLAM SLAM ROCK'N'ROLL

CHATTERBOX
853 VALENCIA
btwn 19th & 20th   821-1891

A ROCK 'N ROLL PARTY 7 DAYS A WEEK
6:00 P.M. - 2:00 A.M.
LIVE MUSIC FRIDAYS SATURDAYS
10:00 PM - 1:30 AM
21 & OVER I.D. REQUIRED

| FRIDAYS | 3/4 Dough Boys FROM CANADA BOSS HOSS | 3/11 HOUSE of WHEELS PROPER SHOES | 3/18 HOUSECOAT PROJECT STUPID BLOODY CABARET | 3/25 RKL NOFX |
| SATURDAYS | 3/5 BENEFIT FOR SCOTT NOIZE BOYZ JACKSON SAINTS PAPA WHEELIE BEAUTY of DOGS | 3/12 GANG WAR (EX-JONESES, MAU MAUS, LAGUNIS) WHITE STAGG | 3/19 BUCK NAKED & the BARE BOTTOM BOYS THE BAR DONKEYS | 3/26 THE RETURN of the MUSKRATS ALSO: BOARD of MACKREL JOHN THAXTON |

WHERE EVERYNITE is TRASH NITE

| BEER WINE SAKE SNAKEBITES | SUN.-THURS. 60oz PITCHERS of MOLSON $4.00 | SUN.-THURS. LONE STAR $1.00 NUKE FOOD | POOL TABLE PINBALL GORE MOVIES No ART |

IGGY : RAMONES : ALICE : DOLLS : DEAD BOYS :
MOTORHEAD : AC/DC :: STONES : THUNDERS

THE WORLD PREMIERE OF
TWITCH
WITH
VERBAL ABUSE

CHATTERBOX
853 VALENCIA, S.F.
21 AND OVER
I-D REQUIRED

10:00 PM
FRIDAY FEBRUARY 19th
INFO: 821-1891

KLUB KOMOTION
2179 16TH St.
PRESENTS A FOOD NOT BOMBS
APRIL 22, 1989
$5.00 CHEAP! BENEFIT WITH
Subtle Plague
Yeastie Girlz
Swollen Boss Toad
Victims Family
& A Puppet Show
P. Ruck 1989

COFFIN BREAK
&
BOMB
SAT.
10 PM   4/9 $3
CHATTERBOX

BOMB
THRENODY
CHATTERBOX SAT AUG 1st

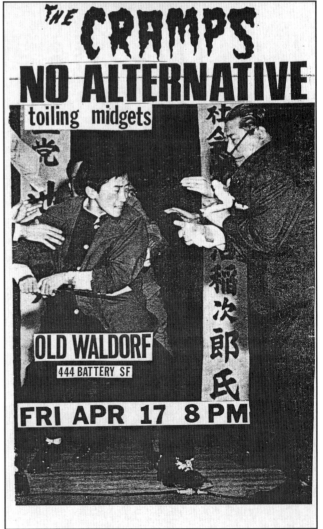

THE CRAMPS
NO ALTERNATIVE
toiling midgets
OLD WALDORF
444 BATTERY SF
FRI APR 17 8 PM

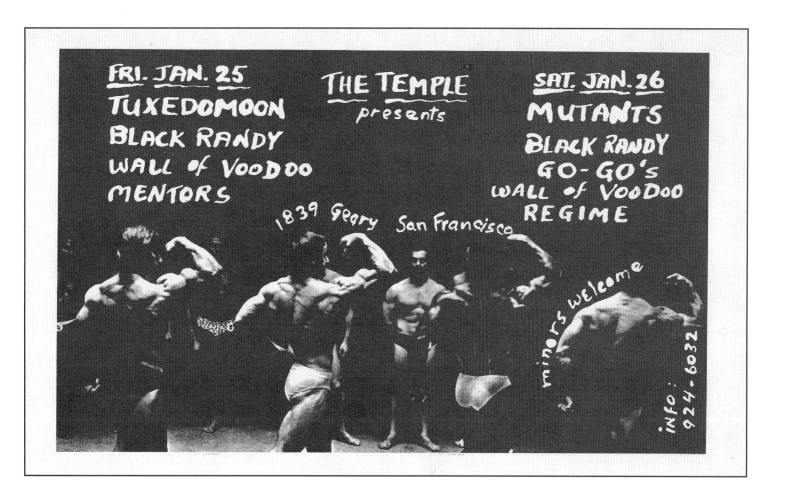

116

MYSTERY TRAIN
WITH KATHY PECK
SF MUSIC WORKS Thurs 5-5
SF MUSIC WORKS Thurs 5-2.6

the Sneetches
cat heads
shower scene
FRIDAY 2/5
MUSIC WORKS
2140 market
9:30pm
$5

SATURDAY NOV. 22
NOISE NACHT · 11

TAO MAO
KATHARSIST
S66 T4

MCS   455 TENTH St.
AT HARRISON
626·7240

SYSTEMS COLLAPSE
18 FEB
CLUB NINE

117

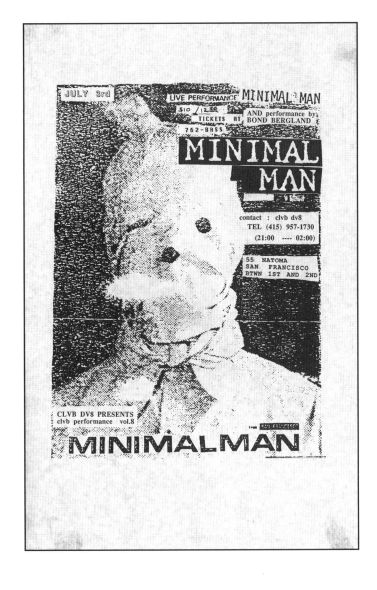

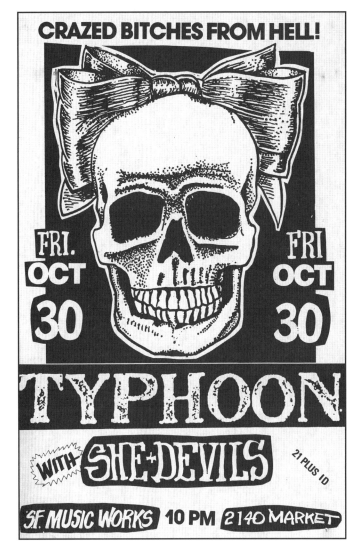

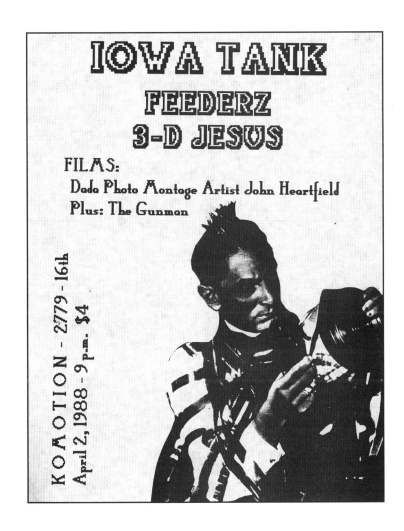

PENELOPE HOUSTON AND THE BIRDBOYS
at the
HOTEL UTAH

NANCIE DE ROSS

KEN and STEVE

COLD BEER HOT CHILI. 4th & BRYANT 10PM 4 BUCK$!

SAT. OCT. 10

FRI. FEB. 29

IMPATIENT
Youth
45's
No ALTERNATIVE
FLIPPER
LEWD

1839 GEARY - SAN FRANCISCO

THE TEMPLE
presents

SAT. MAR. 1

MAGIC
BAND
MUTANTS
UNITS
45's

MINORS WELCOME

MONEY
FRIDAY OCTOBER 9TH 1992
FOR
FILTH
WEEKLY WEIRD NIGHTS
★ MDC ★
BIKINI KILL
FLUFFY T SHIRT BOUTIQUE
plus PUNK ROCK KARAOKE
★ KLUB ★
KOMOTION
2779 16TH
eed: propagate FILTH

CLVB DV8

the return of
TUXEDOMOON
FRIDAY MAY 30TH 9PM

the return of
TUXEDOMOON
FRIDAY MAY 30TH 9PM

"Ship of Fools ... Concert at Home"

FRIDAY MAY 30TH 9PM
TICKETS AVAILABLE AT BASS - 762-BASS

CLVB DV8 540 Howard Street (415) 957-1730

EIN'STUR'ZEN'DE NEU'BAU'TEN
(ĪN'STŬR'ZĚN'DĚ NŎY'BŎW'TĚN) n.
immensely powerful act combining a sense of internal conflict with a societal apocalypse, producing such intense energy that the concept of positive and negative is crushed into rational oblivion; collapsing new buildings; amelodic barrage from sounds of clashing, vibration, and inflammation from the impact of metal on metal and tool on metal; the scraping, beating, and boring of steel springs, sheets and coils, power drills and other construction materials.

EINSTURZENDE NEUBAUTEN

SRL: SURVIVAL
RESEARCH
LABORATORIES

LOTS OF MIRRORS

FRIDAY JUNE 6TH 9PM $15
CLVB DV8 55 NATOMA STREET 957-1730
TICKETS AVAILABLE AT BASS 415-762-BASS
MARK PAULINE, MATT HECKERT, ERIC WERNER

A SHOW ENACTED ENTIRELY
WITH MACHINES, ROBOTS AND
SPECIAL EFFECTS

3 BENEFITS

WED. APRIL 13 8:30 PM
BENEFIT FOR THE NO MORE
CENSORSHIP DEFENSE FUND
The Premiere of the Video Documentary of
Jello Biafra's "Pornography" Trial in
Los Angeles. Featured are statements and
opinions from the defendants and prosecution
inside and outside the courtroom.
THE ZENDIKS live acoustic set
ROB BREZNY from WORLD
ENTERTAINMENT WAR and author of
IMAGES ARE DANGEROUS in a
spoken word performance
$4.00 Donation

SAT. APRIL 16 9:00 PM
BENEFIT FOR LA VICTORIA
SOUP KITCHEN IN
SANTIAGO, CHILE
Featuring a Slide Show on the continued
survival of a Vital Food Program in the
politically repressive atmosphere of Chile.
SISTER DOUBLE HAPPINESS
NOMEANSNO (from Canada)
KAMANCHAKA (Chilean Folk Music)
LICHI FUENTES and Band (Andean Music)
$6.00 Donation

SAT. APRIL 30 9:00 PM
BENEFIT FOR THE BERKELEY
HOMELESS COLLECTIVE
Speakers from 10th Street in Berkeley
PENELOPE HOUSTON
X-TAL, HALF BLIND, BEEF CHURCH
DJ AMAZING GRACE
$5.00 Donation

WHEELCHAIR ACCESSIBLE, MINORS WELCOME
22 FILLMORE LINE TO 16TH AND FOLSOM

2779 SIXTEENTH ST SAN FRANCISCO
KOMOTION

BIRD KILLERS

16TH NOTE

9PM AUG 5

621-1617
3116 - 16TH

SCREAM

NO COVER NO COVER

STIFF LEGGED SHEEP

FROM IOWA CITY, IOWA

GLORIOUS DIN
RAINING HOUSE

ATA
GALLERY
220 8th Street
San Francisco, CA 94103
415/431-8394

AUG 15 FRIDAY

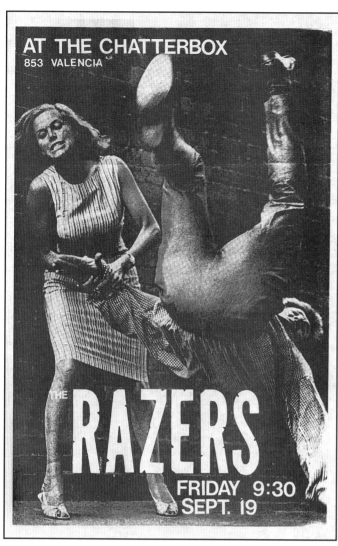

AT THE CHATTERBOX
853 VALENCIA

THE RAZERS
FRIDAY 9:30
SEPT. 19

White Dog PRESENTS

THE RATZ

Wednesday, Aug 24 9pm

Advance Tickets
$2.50

7 MARITIME PLAZA
SAN FRANCISCO, CA 94111

OLD WALDORF

$3.25
at the door

444 BATTERY STREET
SAN FRANCISCO, CA 94111

"SAN FRANCISCO'S PREMIER NIGHT CLUB & RESTAURANT"
PHONE (415) EXBROOK 7-4335

TICKETS CAN BE PURCHASED AT ALL BASS OUTLETS

Photo - Scott Lyons Design - Don Evenson

WILL PORTER
BIRTHDAY
CONCERT
THURS.
JAN. 29
8pm
5.50 adv.

TICKETS AT ALL
BASS
OUTLETS

GUEST STAR
MARY WELLS
24 Hit Records including MY GUY

Plus BUENA VISTA w. terry hutchison

OLD WALDORF
444 BATTERY   clay & washington
MINORS WELCOME

SYSTEMS COLLAPSE

LIPPS UNDERGROUND
9 PM TUESDAY 15 DECEMBER 1987 PIGLATIN

123

THE NAKED INTO   CLUB NINE   FRI. DEC. 5

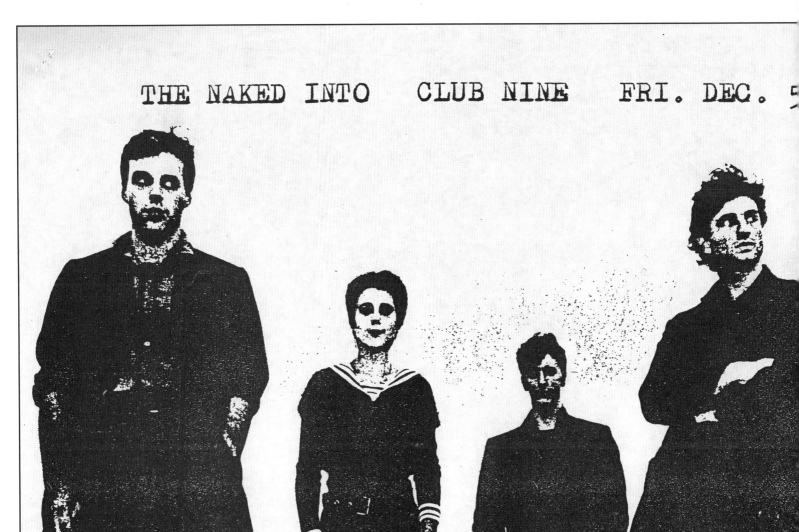

PRAY FOR RAIN
THURS. NOV. 6

399 9th (at Harrison) S.F., CA 94103   863-3291

124

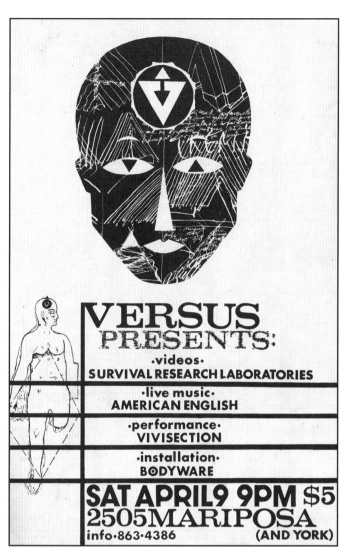

VERSUS
PRESENTS:
·videos·
SURVIVAL RESEARCH LABORATORIES
·live music·
AMERICAN ENGLISH
·performance·
VIVISECTION
·installation·
BODYWARE
SAT APRIL 9 9PM $5
2505 MARIPOSA
info·863·4386   (AND YORK)

VERSUS BENEFIT
SAT 27TH
FEB
9PM

$6

BEATNIGS INDUSTRIAL
RAIN
FOREST
2505 MARIPOSA SF

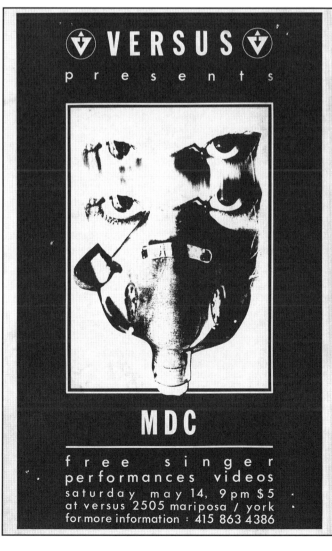

VERSUS
p r e s e n t s

MDC

f r e e   s i n g e r
performances videos
saturday may 14, 9pm $5
at versus 2505 mariposa / york
for more information : 415 863 4386

VERSUS
presents

MISSILE HARMONY
SHARK BAIT
WORLD ENTERTAINMENT WAR

9 P.M. $5

SAT.
APRIL 30
2505 MARIPOSA
info·863·4386   (AND YORK)

WED., AUG. 26

M-1 ALTERNATIVE

"if you only knew"

PHOTO: RICO

NIGHTBREAK

mekons
FROM THE UK

THURSDAY JUNE 26TH 9PM

WITH
NEW YORK PERFORMANCE ARTISTS
KAREN FINLEY & LYDIA LUNCH
THE FINAL REVENGE OF THE ULTIMATE P#?!Y KILLERS
$12.50/$15.00 TICKETS AVAILABLE BASS
415---762---BASS
CLVB DV8
55 natoma street btwn 1st & 2nd

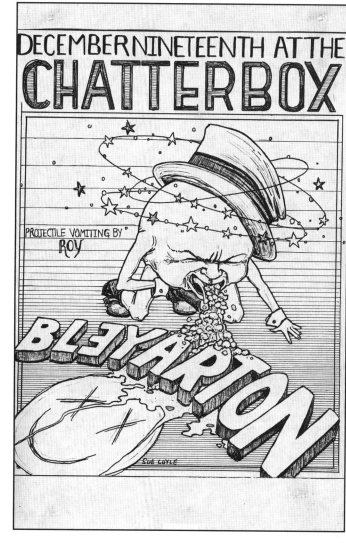

DECEMBERNINETEENTH AT THE
CHATTERBOX

PROJECTILE VOMITING BY ROY

BLEYARTON

SUE COYLE

HAPPY FUCKING VALENTINES DAY

LETHAL GOSPEL
with
TOUCH ME HOOKER
AT Chatterbox

saturday
february 14, 1987
10:30 p.m.

853 VALENCIA ST.
(betw. 19k & 20th) only $3.00

ALSO: FEB 28th at HOTEL UTAH (4th & BRYANT st.) 10:30 & 12:30 $2.00

SNAKEFINGER

in CONCERT

Snakefinger's
Vestal Virgins

Night of
Desirable
Objects

with special guest
NOVA MOB
CLVB DV8
55 NATOMA SF TIX @BASS
SATURDAY, MAY 15TH 9PM

127

TERRA INCOGNITA IN A RECORD RELEASE PARTY FOR PENELOPE HOUSTON WITH THE LONGSHOREMEN

NINE NINTH & HARRISON THURS. SEPT. 25

JOHN SEX
THURS. DEC. 18 10pm
KITTY & CYCLE SOUL BLUES

NINE
399 9th (at Harrison) S.F. CA 94103 863-3291

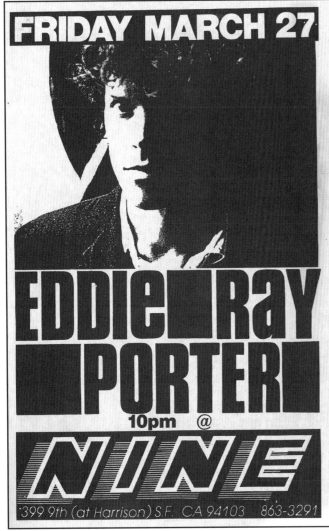

FRIDAY MARCH 27

EDDIE RAY PORTER
10pm @
NINE
399 9th (at Harrison) S.F. CA 94103 863-3291

CHRIS ISAAK

CHRIS ISAAK
SAT. MARCH 7th 10 PM.
SPECIAL 18 and OVER SHOW—
SUNDAY MARCH 8TH 5 PM SHARP.

NINE
399 9th (at Harrison) S.F. CA 94103 863-3291

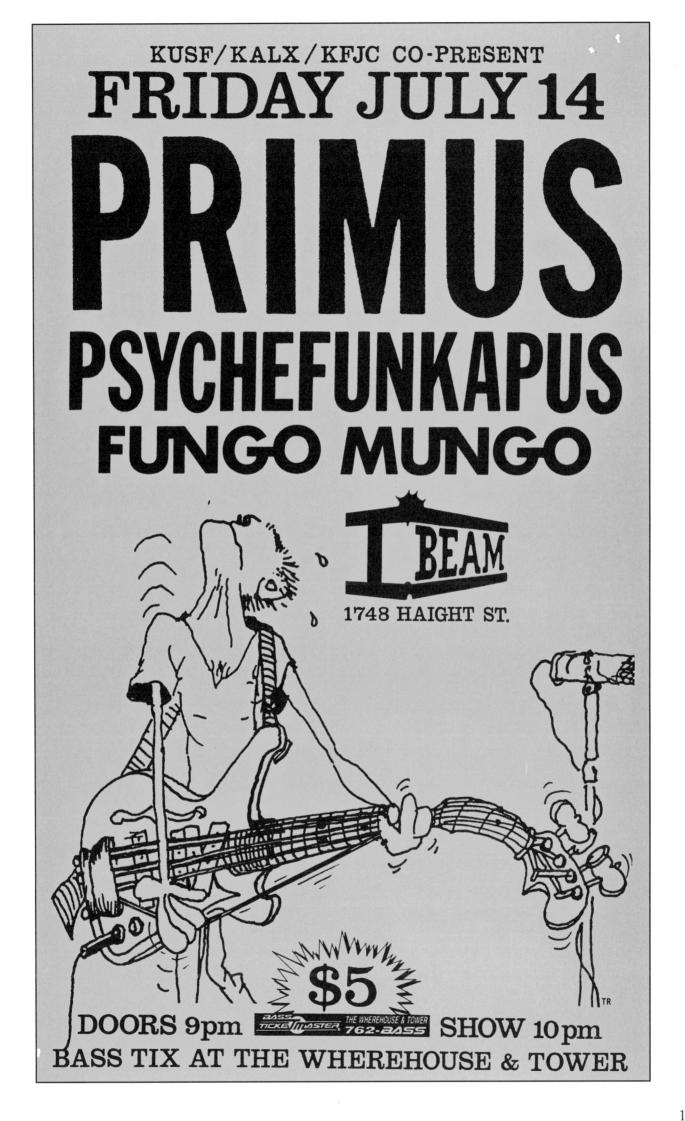

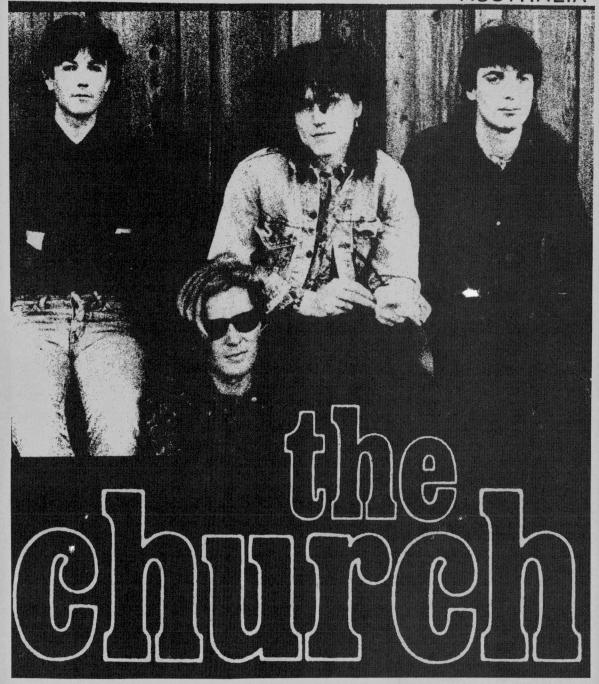

TUES. AUG. 5

KUSF/KALX CO-ANNOUNCE
BAY AREA EXCLUSIVE

FROM AUSTRALIA

the church

DOORS OPEN 7:30
SHOW: 9 P.M.

ADVANCE TIX AT
ROUGH TRADE,
REVOLVER, I BEAM
AQUARIUS, RECKLESS
& DALJEETS

AUG. 11 - BUTTHOLE SURFERS
SCRATCH ACID

1748 HAIGHT ST

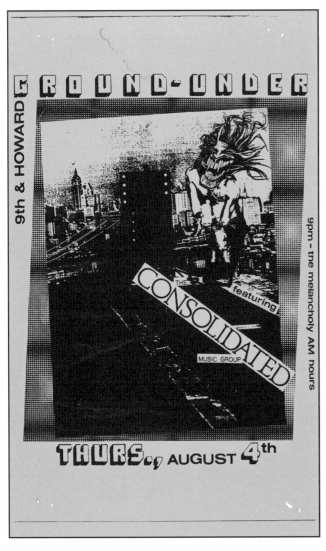

GROUND-UNDER

9th & HOWARD

9pm - the melancholy AM hours

featuring

THE CONSOLIDATED

MUSIC GROUP

THURS., AUGUST 4th

NIGHTBREAK

wed 6
BLUE MOVIE
THE WHITEFRONTS

thr 7
ALLEYBOYS
BLUE WEST

fri 8
SPANISH ELVIS

KUSF/KALX CO-PRESENT
A BAY AREA EXCLUSIVE
MONDAY JAN.4

REVOLTING COCKS

FEATURING

AL JOURGENSEN, BILL REIFLIN & ION
OF MINISTRY
NIVEK OGRE
OF SKINNY PUPPY
LUC VAN ACKER

I BEAM

1748 HAIGHT ST.

DOORS 9pm
ADVANCE TIX AT
I-BEAM, REVOLVER
RECKLESS
ROUGH TRADE
HALL OF RECORDS
AQUARIUS & BASS

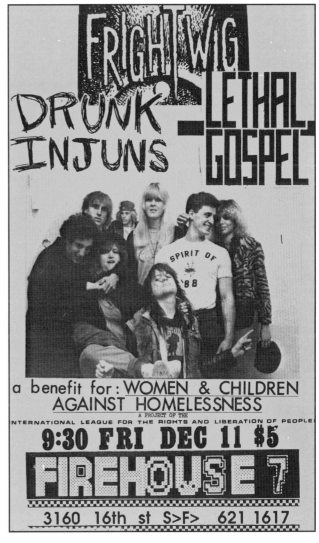

FRIGHT WIG
DRUNK INJUNS
LETHAL GOSPEL

a benefit for: WOMEN & CHILDREN
AGAINST HOMELESSNESS
A PROJECT OF THE
INTERNATIONAL LEAGUE FOR THE RIGHTS AND LIBERATION OF PEOPLE
9:30 FRI DEC 11 $5
FIREHOUSE 7
3160 16th st S>F>   621 1617

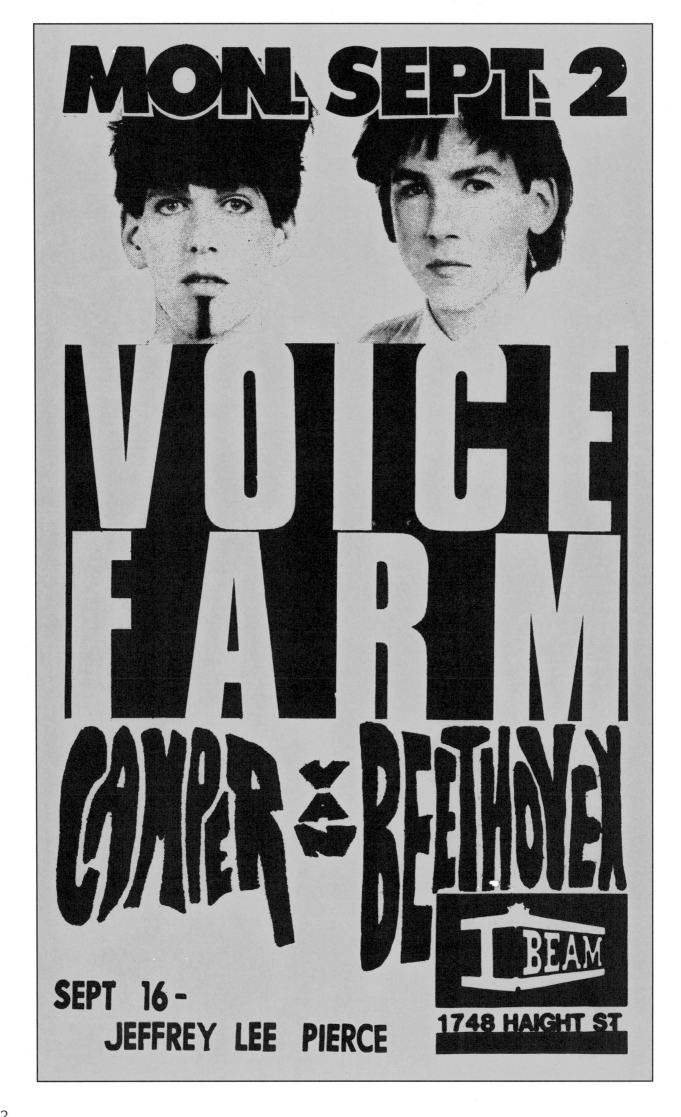

MON. SEPT. 2

VOICE FARM

CAMPER BEETHOVEN

BEAM

SEPT 16 –
JEFFREY LEE PIERCE

1748 HAIGHT ST

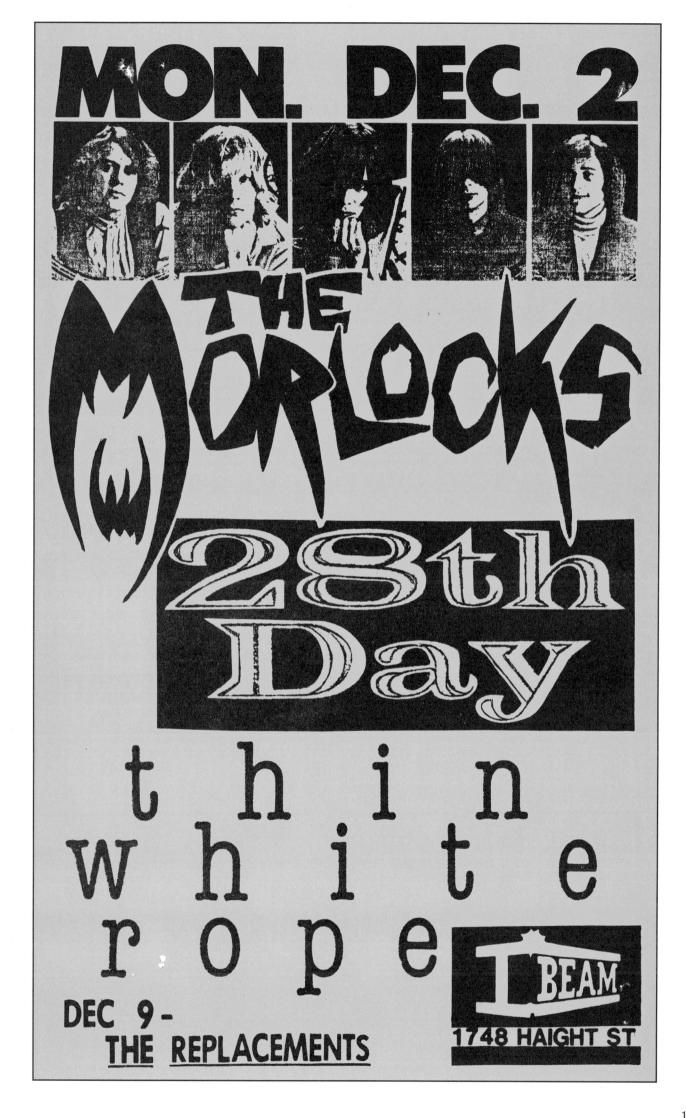

MON. DEC. 2

THE Morlocks

28th Day

thin white rope

DEC 9 -
THE REPLACEMENTS

I BEAM
1748 HAIGHT ST

133

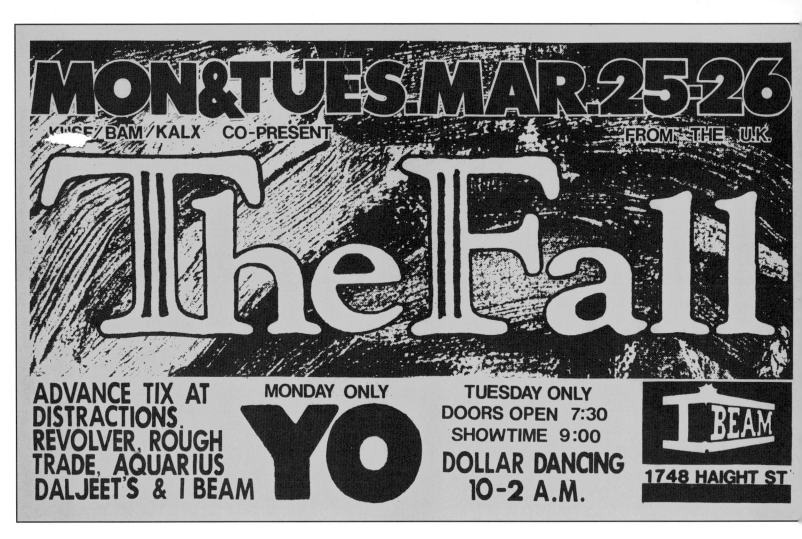

MON & TUES. MAR. 25-26

KUSF/BAM/KALX CO-PRESENT

FROM THE U.K.

The Fall

ADVANCE TIX AT DISTRACTIONS, REVOLVER, ROUGH TRADE, AQUARIUS DALJEET'S & I BEAM

MONDAY ONLY YO

TUESDAY ONLY
DOORS OPEN 7:30
SHOWTIME 9:00
DOLLAR DANCING 10-2 A.M.

I BEAM
1748 HAIGHT ST.

DM DEAD MARILYN

KENNEL CLUB

SAT. 26 SEPT.

Feast

SUNDAY
NOV 1
FRIDAY
NOV 13

NIGHT
BREAK

1821 HAIGHT STREET

MON. OCT. 21

KUSF/KALX
CO-PRESENT   6TH ANNIVERSARY PARTY

HOODOO GURUS

Gene Loves Jezebel

ADVANCE TIX AT I BEAM
ROUGH TRADE, AQUARIUS,
REVOLVER, & DALJEET'S
OCT 28 - THE LYRES

I BEAM
1748 HAIGHT ST

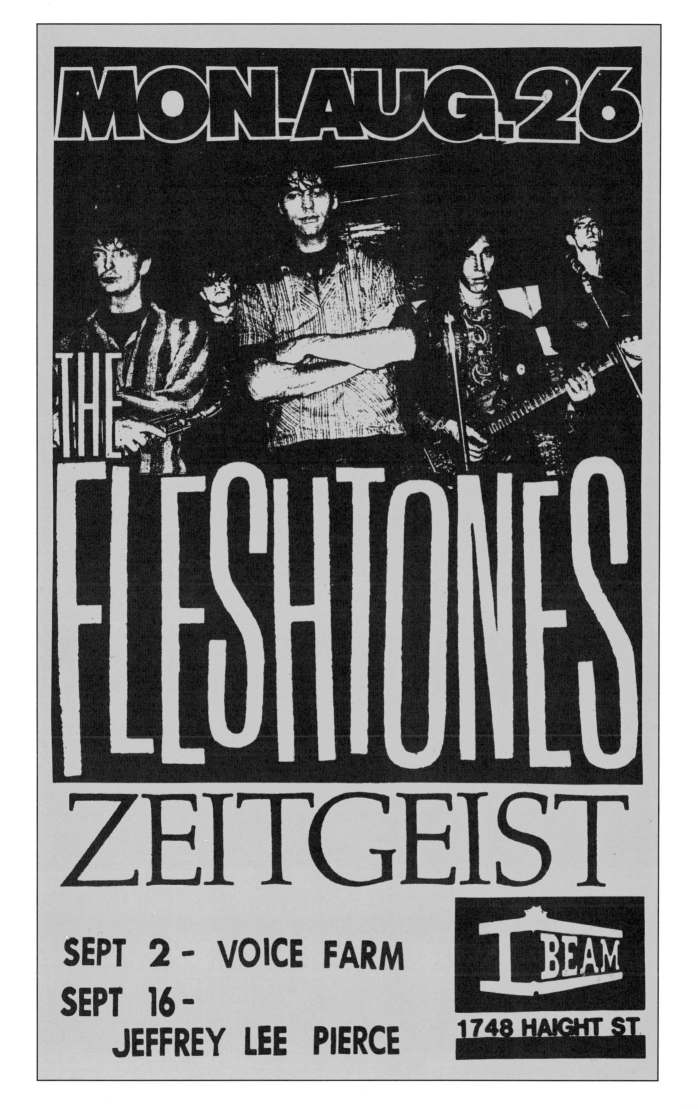

MON. AUG. 26

THE FLESHTONES

ZEITGEIST

SEPT 2 - VOICE FARM
SEPT 16 -
JEFFREY LEE PIERCE

I BEAM
1748 HAIGHT ST.

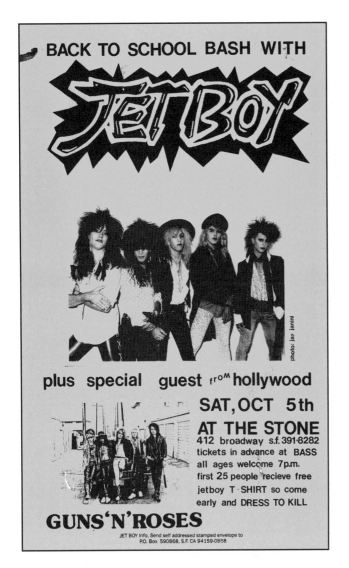

BACK TO SCHOOL BASH WITH

JETBOY

plus special guest from hollywood

SAT, OCT 5th
AT THE STONE
412 broadway s.f. 391-8282
tickets in advance at BASS
all ages welcome 7p.m.
first 25 people recieve free
jetboy T-SHIRT so come
early and DRESS TO KILL

GUNS 'N' ROSES

JET BOY Info, Send self addressed stamped envelope to
P.O. Box 590868, S.F. CA 94159-0858

photo: Jay Janini

D.O.A.

Tickets available at Bass Ticket Centers, including Record Factory

Bring Back the Future

TOUR '85

and from england
CONFLICT

IN THE LOBBY DURING THE SHOW
A.M.E.S.
ACTION FOR ANIMALS
NO BUSINESS AS USUAL
BOUND TOGETHER BOOKS
JOHN BROWN ANTI-KLAN
COMMITTEE

the farm
1499 potrero
doors 7p.m.

431-1326

CHRIST ON PARADE
THE WITNESSES
thursday
august 8
at army st.
early show

tickets $5 advance at TICKETRON

WE DON'T NEED UNITY... WE NEED CO-OPERATION

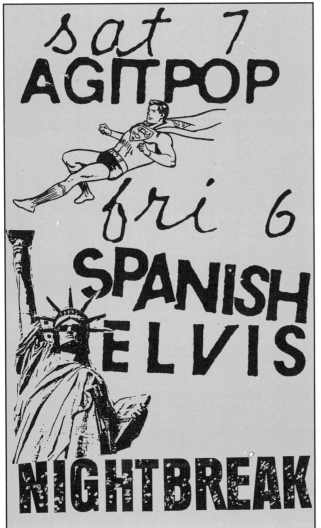

sat 7
AGITPOP

fri 6
SPANISH
ELVIS

NIGHTBREAK

DanceVision Presents
San Francisco Musicians, Dancers & Visual Artists in

Night at the Palace

A Première Multi-Media Event

Featuring
The Nuns
Bar Wars Ballet
Third Wave Dance Theatre
Cecelia-Marie Bowman
Céce Chévere

Blanche Brown
Dancers Working
Ava & André
Ken Blakey
Ron Petersen

Saturday & Sunday ■ June 29, 30 ■ 8 p.m.
Admission ■ $9 Door, $8 Advance
Ticket Information ■ 921-9968, BASS
Palace of Fine Arts Theatre ■ 3301 Lyon at Lombard ■ (next to Exploratorium)

Tickets available at Bass Ticket Centers, including Record Factory. Charge by phone: (415) 762-BASS

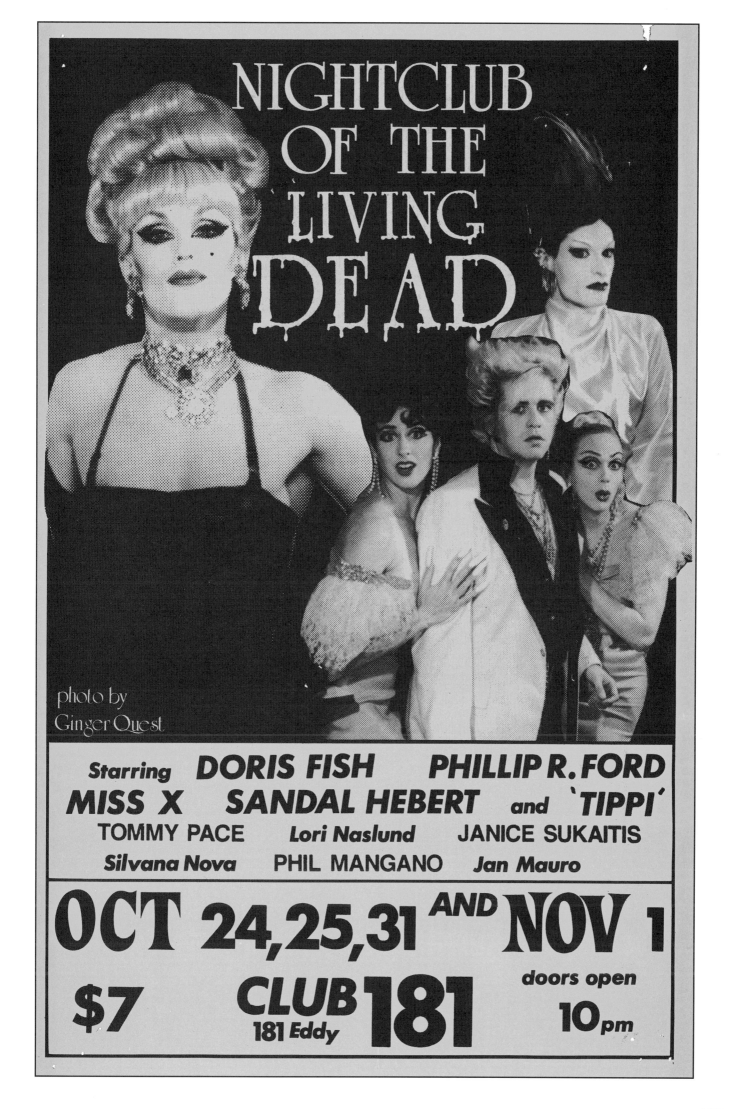

139

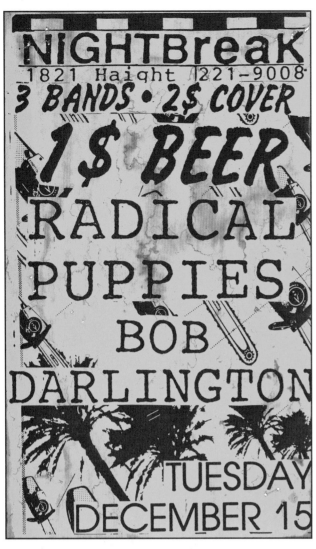

NiGHTBreak
1821 Haight 221-9008
3 BANDS • 2$ COVER
1 $ BEER
RADICAL
PUPPIES
BOB
DARLINGTON
TUESDAY
DECEMBER 15

JANE COUNTY
BUCK NAKED
& THE BAREBOTTOM BOYS

TREAT HER RIGHT

KENNEL CLUB
628 DIVISADERO

FRIDAY JAN. 8
DOORS OPEN 9:00
SHOWTIME 10:00
$6.00 AT THE DOOR
TICKETS AVAILABLE AT BASS

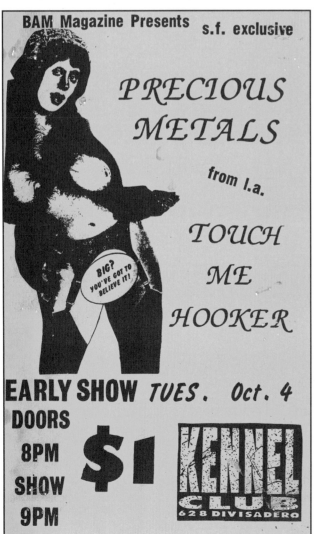

BAM Magazine Presents   s.f. exclusive

PRECIOUS METALS
from l.a.
TOUCH ME HOOKER

BIG? YOU'VE GOT TO BELIEVE IT!

EARLY SHOW TUES. Oct. 4
DOORS 8PM
SHOW 9PM
$1
KENNEL CLUB
628 DIVISADERO

NiGHTBreak
1821 Haight 221-9008
3 BANDS • DOLLAR BEER
TRIM
CASUAL ITALIANS
BOB DARLINGTON
TUES. 29 SEPT 2$

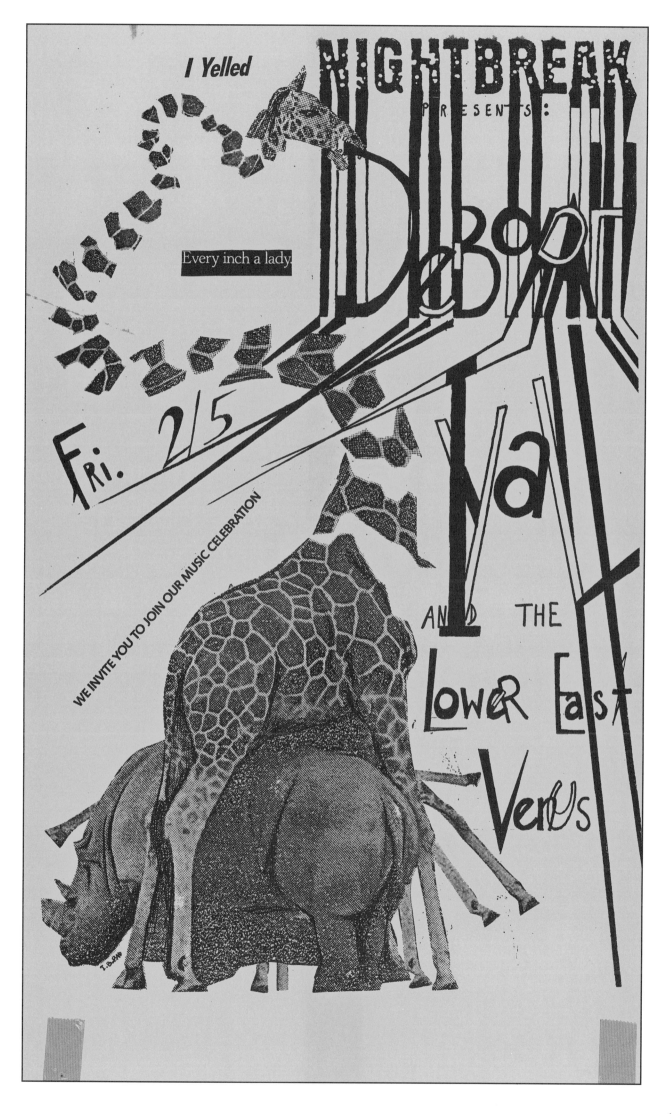

141

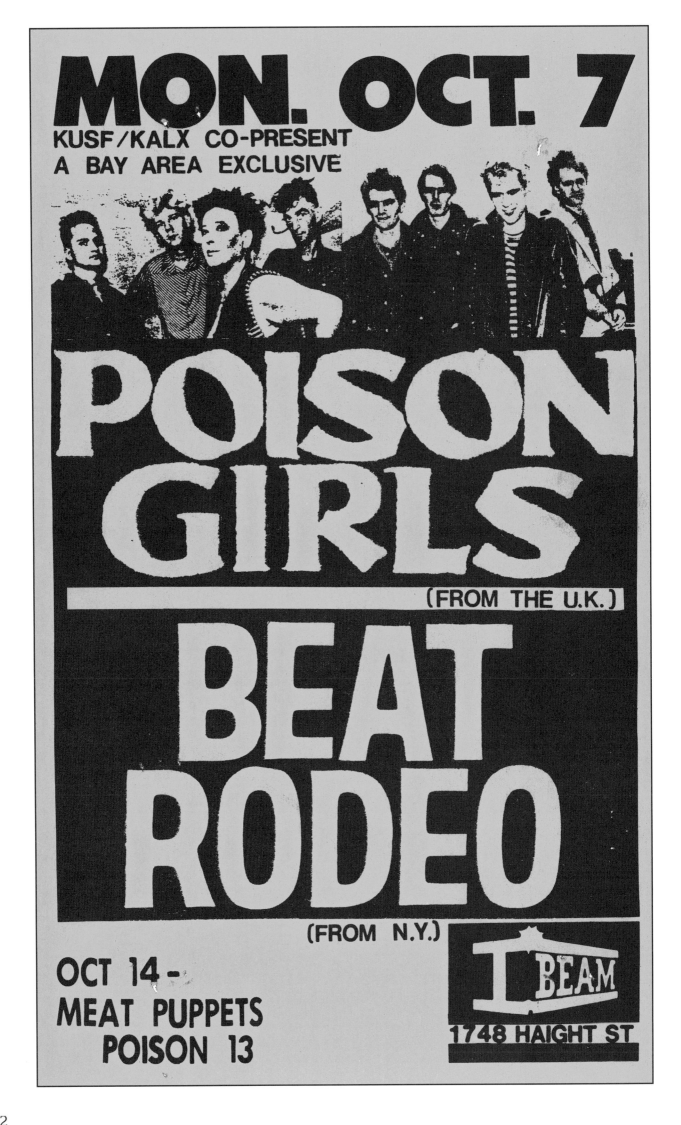

MON. OCT. 7
KUSF/KALX CO-PRESENT
A BAY AREA EXCLUSIVE

POISON
GIRLS
(FROM THE U.K.)

BEAT
RODEO
(FROM N.Y.)

OCT 14 -
MEAT PUPPETS
POISON 13

I BEAM
1748 HAIGHT ST

142

LOVE CLUB
MATTE BLACK
(EX-CRAWL AWAY MACHINE)

KENNEL CLUB
628 DIVISADERO

**THURSDAY,
OCTOBER 15
10:30 sharp**

NIGHTBREAK
1821 HAIGHT   221-9008

MY
SIN

Fri.
September 13

THE MORLOCKS
WITH
THE MIRACLE WORKERS
THE SEA HAGS

SAT.   **SEPT. 28**

BROTHERHOOD FILM

M.C.: JERRY CORNELIUS
D.J.: BARRY ST. VITUS (K·ALX)
SWEEDISH·AMERICAN HALL 2174 MARKET ST.
9:00 PM
ALL AGES/FULL BAR   6$

DEXTER·DE·VOE

NIGHTBREAK
SATURDAY, APRIL 16

144

145

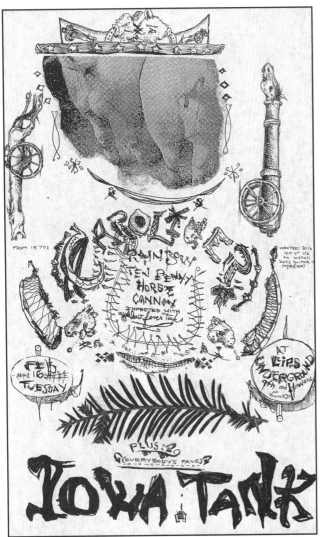

146

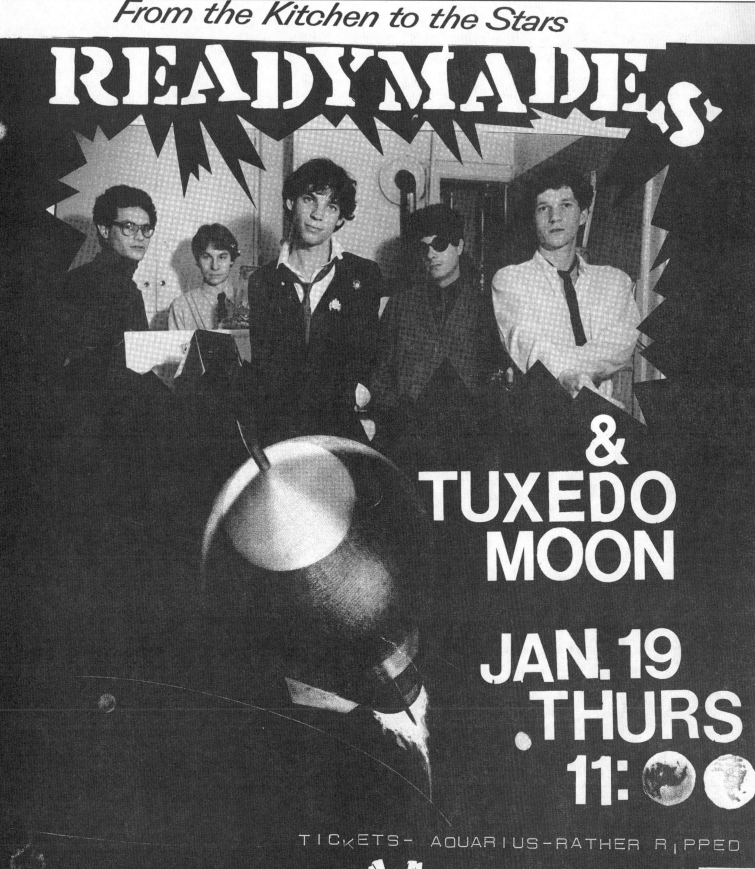

From the Kitchen to the Stars

READYMADES

& TUXEDO MOON

JAN. 19 THURS 11:

TICKETS- AQUARIUS-RATHER RIPPED

443 BROADWAY SAN FRANCISCO **MABUHAY GARDENS** TELEPHONE (415) 956 3315

A DIRKSEN-MILLER PRODUCTION

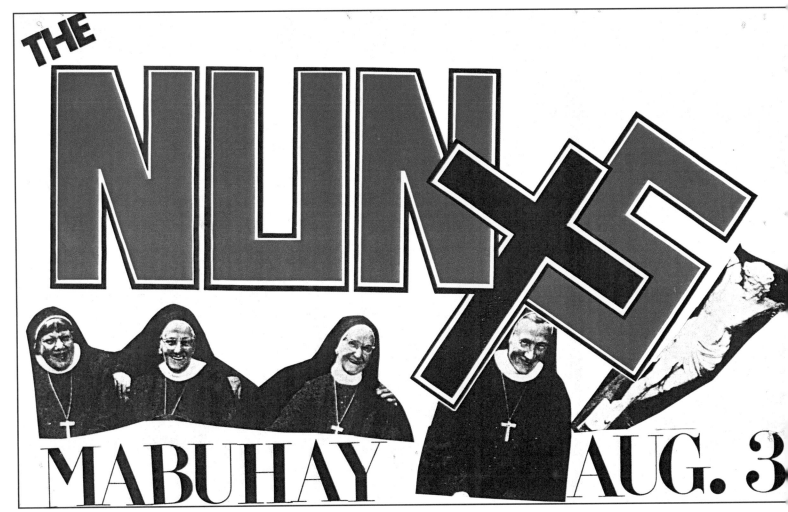

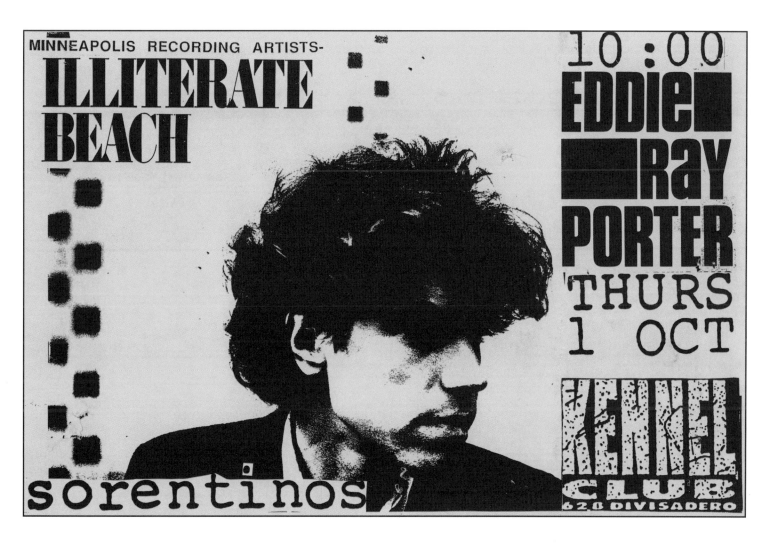

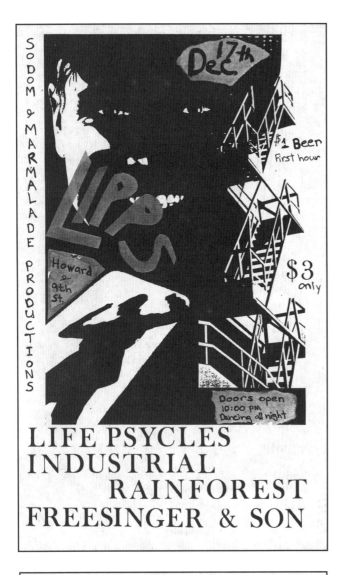

**LIFE PSYCLES
INDUSTRIAL
RAINFOREST
FREESINGER & SON**

tuesday august 11, 1987

ARCHIPELAGO
BREWING
CO.

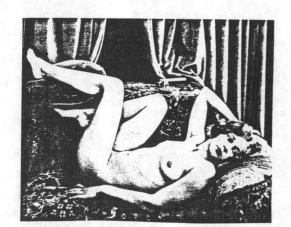

LIVE ON STAGE
at LIPPS UNDERGROUND club

NINTH AND HOWARD st.

$3   DOORS OPEN 9pm

DEATH IS EVERYWHERE

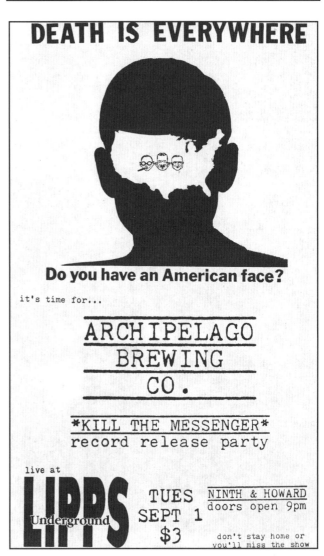

Do you have an American face?

it's time for...

ARCHIPELAGO
BREWING
CO.

KILL THE MESSENGER
record release party

live at **LIPPS** Underground   TUES SEPT 1 $3   NINTH & HOWARD doors open 9pm

don't stay home or
you'll miss the show

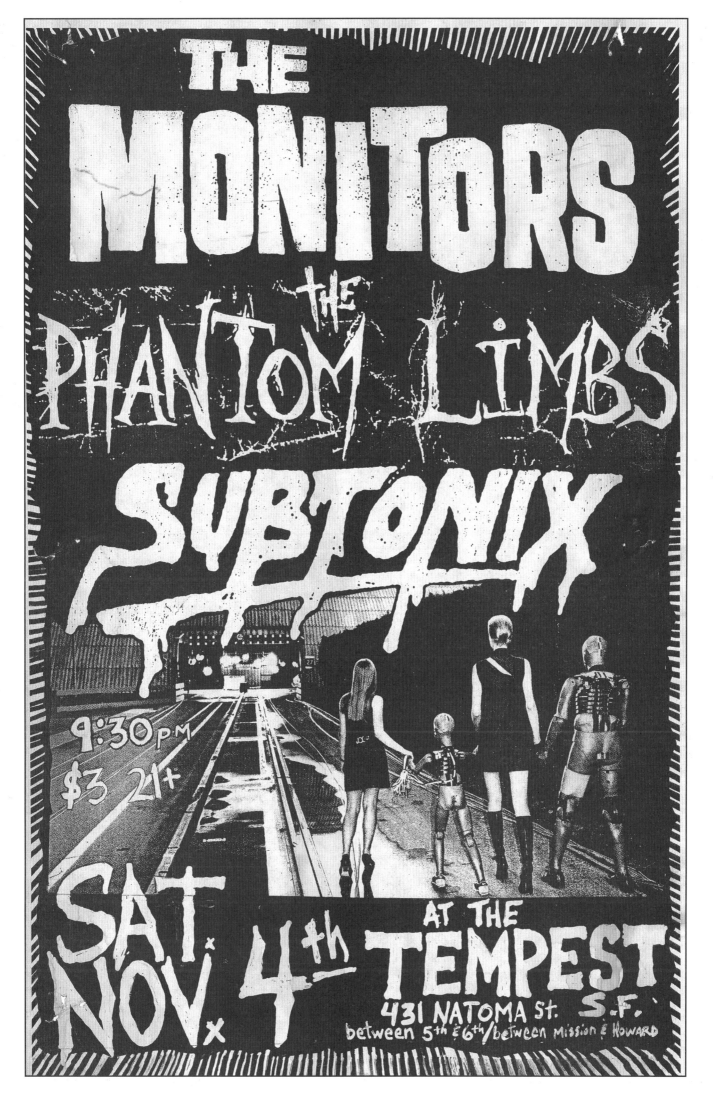

151

NIGHTBReaK
THRILL
OF THE
PULL

FRIDAY
31 JULY

BORMAN 6
NIGHTBReaK
12/4/87   4$

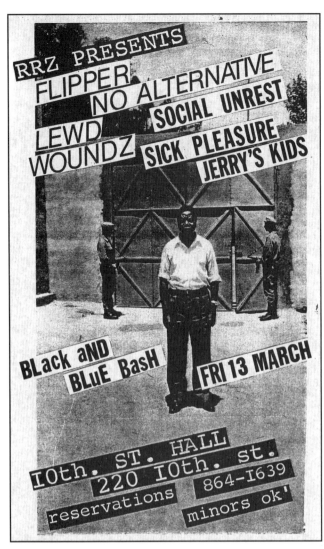

RRZ PRESENTS
FLIPPER
NO ALTERNATIVE
LEWD   SOCIAL UNREST
WOUNDZ   SICK PLEASURE
        JERRY'S KIDS

BLack aND BLuE BasH   FRI 13 MARCH

10th. ST. HALL
220 10th. st.
reservations   864-1639
minors ok'

MADNESS

from ENGLAND

At Aquarius Records 595 CASTRO
WED. March 12 5:00 PM

MADNESS
ONE STEP BEYOND..

SEE THEM AT THE OLD WALDORF MARCH 12-8:00

MADNESS

KILL THE MESSENGER

"When You Meet the Buddha..."

TUESDAY
SEPT 1
LIPPS
201 9th ST

9:30 PM
$3

TO MARK
OUR NEW
ALBUM

with
HIPPIE
TEMPTATION
from L.A.

JORMA
SOLO ACOUSTIC BLUES

FRIDAY, MARCH 9
10:30 P.M.

At LA CITTA
571 MISSION ST. (at 2nd)
San Francisco • 957-1166

PRIMUS with
SLOVENLY
SAT - MAY III AT
GRAFFITI

2 NIGHTS ONLY IN SF!
FRI SAT MARCH 20, 21

LOS MICROWAVES

LE DISKE FRI

VALENCIA
TOOL & DIE
SAT

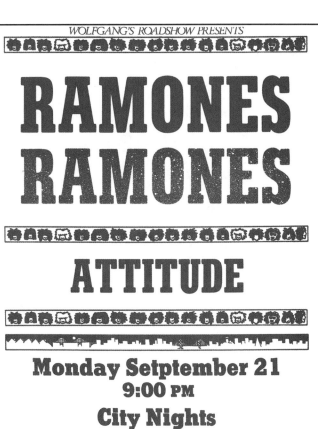

WOLFGANG'S ROADSHOW PRESENTS

RAMONES
RAMONES

ATTITUDE

Monday Setptember 21
9:00 PM

City Nights
715 Harrison St.

All Ages Welcome
Tickets At All Bass Outlets

DNA LOUNGE

WED. DEC. 3
Holiday Extravaganza With

THE
TUBES

and special guest
COMBINATION GO
Featuring **Mingo**
Tickets $10 At Door

375 11th Street   626-1409

DIRECT FROM ENGLAND

CHRIS and COSEY
OF THROBBING GRISTLE

BAY AREA EXCLUSIVE

WITH CLUB FOOT ORCHESTRA

THURSDAY MAY 8

wolfgang's
WOLFGANGS 901 COLUMBUS ST, SF.
DOORS 8PM SHOW 9PM
ADV. TIX THROUGH ALL BASS OUTLETS INCLUDING WOLFGANGS BOX OFFICE
FOR MORE INFORMATION (415) 474-2995

THE DNA LOUNGE
375 11TH STREET 626-1409

SUNDAY, MAY 1ST
KUSF BENEFIT FOR THE
"GERM COMPILATION"
FEATURING
PRIMUS
ESKIMO
SORDID HUMOR
CARNIVAL LAW
MUD PUPPIES
DOORS OPEN AT 6PM SHOW AT 7 $4 ADMISSION

SUNDAY, MAY 8TH
EVERY MOTHER'S NIGHTMARE
CONSOLIDATED
WITH ADAM SHERBURNE
BOORMAN 6
DOORS OPEN AT 7PM SHOW AT 8 $2 ADMISSION

TRAGIC MULATTO
FUCK BUBBLE
VOMIT LAUNCH

August 1   Hotel Utah

STEVIE STILETTO

☮ is for 🐱
Peace is for Pussies
TOUR 89'
AT THE CHATTERBOX   MARCH

contraband

patriarchy?

STUPID
BLOODY
CABARET
10:30 PM   March 18th
At the CHATTERBOX
Also HOUSECOAT PROJECT!

theater artaud

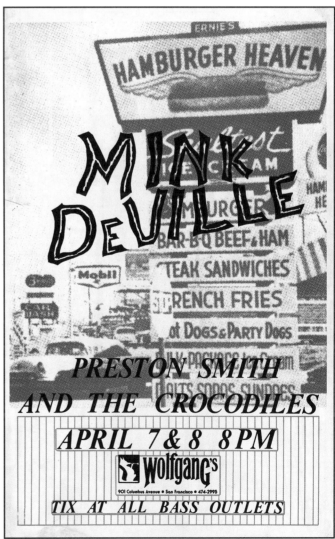

HAMBURGER HEAVEN

MINK DeVILLE

PRESTON SMITH
AND THE CROCODILES
APRIL 7 & 8   8PM
Wolfgang's
901 Columbus Avenue • San Francisco • 474-2995
TIX AT ALL BASS OUTLETS

CLUB WINO PRESENTS

ST. VITAS DAY DANCE

WITH
SOLDIERS OF FORTUNE
SMASHED WEEKEND
SEA HAGS
FAITH NO MORE

SAT. SEPT. 21

Advance Tickets at BASS or at the door

SWEDISH AMERICAN HALL
2174 Market S.F.
between church & castro
8 PM
VIDEOS BY: CLUB GENERIC
LIGHTS BY: BROTHERHOOD OF LIGHT

DJ (not a dj) LEBOWITZ marks the 1st anniversary of his accident with the

D.J. LEBOWITZ
NOT a disc jockey
SCREAM—ALONG !!

9:07 PM SAT AUGUST 31 1985

I WOULD NEVER HURT THE PIANO THE PLAYER!

at SWEDISH·AMERICAN HALL
2174 MARKET/15th San Francisco

ALSO:
• MORLOCKS
• FOUR GIVEN AND
• YARD TRAUMA

BROTHERHOOD OF LIGHT

$6. AT THE DOOR. ALL AGES WELCOME

WED MAY 11

FROM PORTLAND

SLACK*

SAN FRANCISCO MUSIC WORKS

WRESTLING WORMS

SANTA CRUZ

APRIL 30 SAT.
CRYSTAL PISTOL
20th & VALENCIA
SAT
JOE MAMA
ROCKS THE MISSION
w/ FEMME FATALES
SF = DEF
10:30

ZEITGEIST

PARTY WITH the NICK GRAVENITES BAND

9:00 Thursday 9:00

DECEMBER 5

at THE

16th NOTE

3160 16th Street   San Francisco

FORMER MEMBERS OF:

THE ELECTRIC FLAG

QUICKSILVER MESSENGER SERVICE

COMMANDER CODY AND HIS LOST
PLANET AIRMEN

WEASLE AND HOUSECOAT PROJ.

Jill Krementz

9:00 FOLSOM and 8th
at the Baybrick   wed. NOV. 13
CONTINGENT

TWO YEAR ANNIVERSARY PARTY
FOR THE
SEA HAGS
WITH
CELEBRITY SKIN
AND SURPRISE GUEST !!

FRI. MAY 15   DOOR OPENS 9:30 PM
SOUND OF MUSIC
162 TURK   21 + OVER I.D. REQUIRED
SORRY, NO MINORS
FOR MORE INFO: 431-1326 or
567-0103

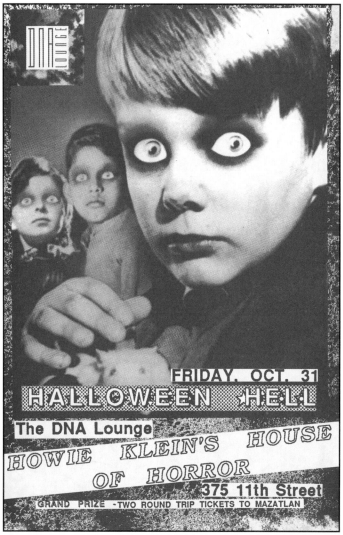

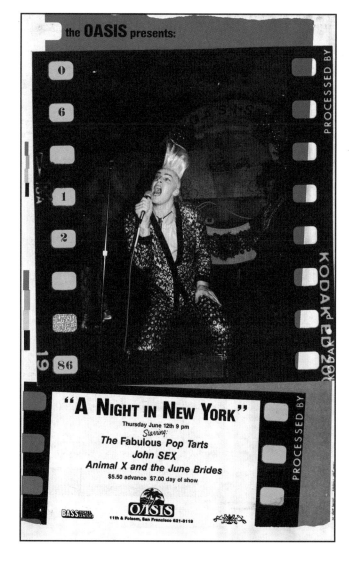

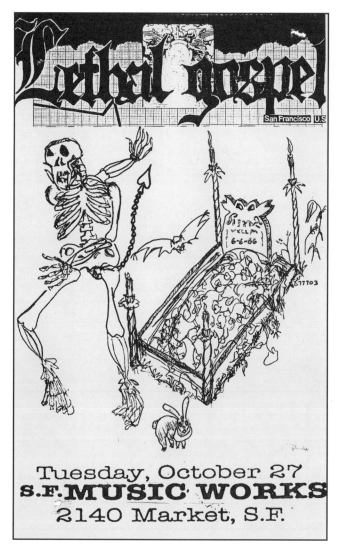

Lethal gospel

San Francisco U.S.

Tuesday, October 27
S.F. MUSIC WORKS
2140 Market, S.F.

NIGHTBREAK

HARD RAIN & The Best Kissers in the World

you wouldn't wanna SLEEP through THESE ones! ...trust me

wed. 8th

fri. 10th

SHIVA DANCIN & the Comic Book Opera

SPEEDWAY RECORDS

NIGHTBreaK
1821 Haight 221-9008

FRI. JULY 15
BOHEMIAN LUV JONES
♠ ♥ ♦ ♣
and
SHE DEVILS

DOOR 9pm 4$

SPEEDWAY RECORDS

SQUIRMING BITCHES PRODUCTIONS
CORDIALLY INVITES YOU TO AN EVENING WITH:
MORALLY BANKRUPT
BURNING WITCHES
CRASH 'N BURN
TYPHOON

MAY 17 9PM CLUB FOOT
at the corner of 3RD & 22ND Sts. Buses: 15 Third, 22 Fillmore

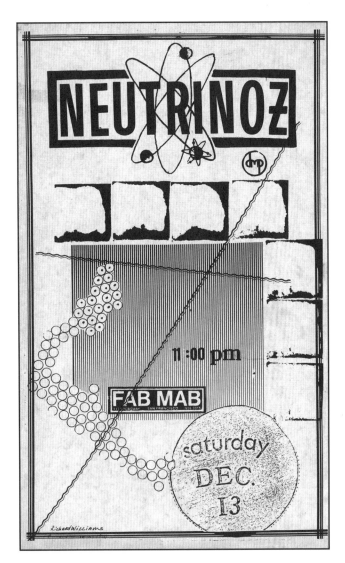

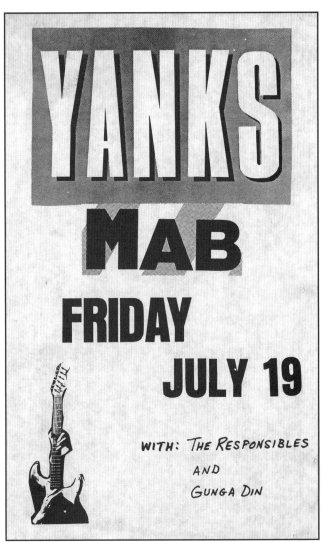

SLIMM
PRODUCTIONS
Presents:
GALA PARTY AT MABUHAY GARDENS
SUNDAY AUGUST 28, 1977 • 10:00 P.M. • FREE BUFFET

MUSIC BY:

Waterbaby

Killerwatt

Kid Courage

$3.00 Cover

SPECIAL GUEST:
Mary Monday

THE CAT HEADS

STEVE WYNN OF THE DREAM SYNDICATE

PAT THOMAS

KENNEL CLUB
628 DIVISADERO

SATURDAY DEC. 19
DOORS OPEN 9:00
SHOWTIME 10:00
$5.00 AT THE DOOR
TICKETS AVAILABLE AT BASS

L.A. GUNS
SAN FRANCISCO EXCLUSIVE

FROM L.A. JUNKYARD
FALLEN ANGEL

KENNEL CLUB
628 DIVISADERO

SATURDAY JAN. 9
DOORS OPEN 9:00
SHOWTIME 10:00
$6.00 AT THE DOOR
TICKETS AVAILABLE AT BASS

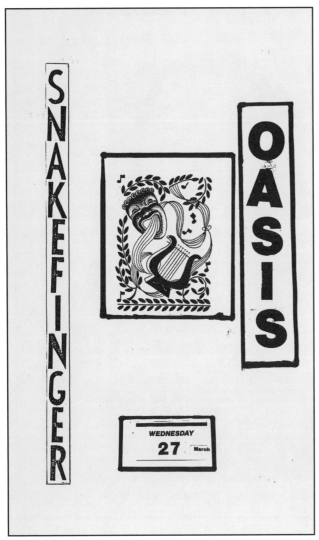

SNAKEFINGER

OASIS

WEDNESDAY
27 March

THE KENNEL CLUB CELEBRATES CALENDAR MAGAZINE'S 6TH ANNIVERSARY WITH A CHRISTMAS BLOWOUT FEATURING:

FLYING COLOR
BUCK NAKED
& THE BAREBOTTOM BOYS
FLOPHOUSE

KENNEL CLUB
628 DIVISADERO

WED. DECEMBER 23
DOORS OPEN 9:00
SHOWTIME 10:00
AT THE DOOR
TICKETS AVAILABLE AT BASS

FREE!

WEDNESDAYS
JANUARY 11

CATETWAUL

THE BIRDKILLERS

DOORS 9pm
SHOW 10:30pm

I BEAM

A KUSF
CO-
PRESENTATION

1748 HAIGHT ST.

MARTIN WEBER GALLERY

PRESENTS
SOUND/PERFORMANCE/VIDEO

POISON GAS RESEARCH
(EXPERIMENTAL ELECTRONICS)

BLACK SWANS
(GREEK ACOUSTIC)

A DOKEY BREATHES, BEAT AND
SPITS AT YOUR SKULL BELL
"DULUOZ IS DEAD.
LONG LIVE DULUOZ."

SEPTEMBER 21ST 10 PM

MARTIN WEBER GALLERY
220 8TH & HOWARD
$3 DONATION
431-8394

one
INCREDIBLY
LARGE
BREAST

APPEARING AT ATA's
LUCKY 7 BENEFIT
777 VALENCIA
SAT. JUNE 11, 1988

9:00 P.M.

ROCK & ROLL
RODEO

SAT. APR.
19. 8:00 PM
362 CAPP
BETWEEN 18TH & 19TH

GRAND FOLLY
PRODUCTION
COMPANY
-present-

HANGING PARTY
with
CODE OF THE WEST
BOSS HOSS G.T. JESUS

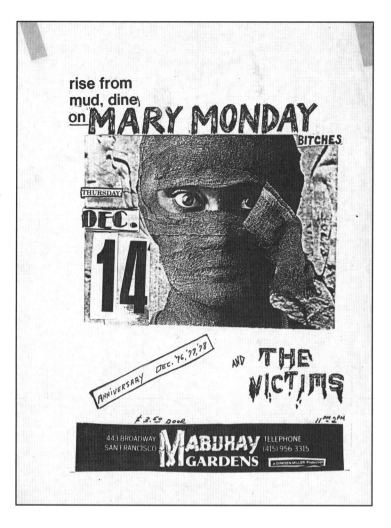

rise from
mud, dine
on **MARY MONDAY**
                              BITCHES

THURSDAY

DEC. 14

Anniversary *Dec. '76,'77,'78*   and **THE VICTIMS**

$3.50 DOOR   11 PM 2PM

443 BROADWAY
SAN FRANCISCO **MABUHAY GARDENS** TELEPHONE
(415) 956 3315
A DIRKSEN-MILLER Production

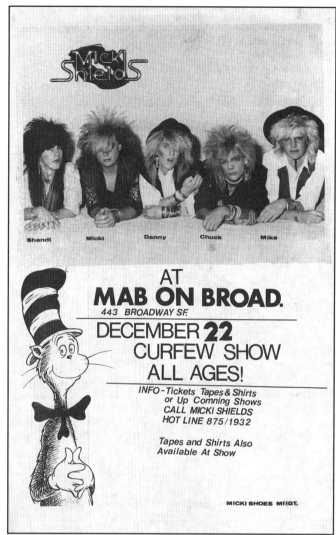

MICKI SHIELDS

Shandi   Micki   Danny   Chuck   Mike

AT
MAB ON BROAD.
443 BROADWAY SF.

DECEMBER 22
CURFEW SHOW
ALL AGES!

INFO-Tickets Tapes & Shirts
or Up Comning Shows
CALL MICKI SHIELDS
HOT LINE 875/1932

Tapes and Shirts Also
Available At Show

MICKI SHOES MNGT.

SIN
®

IS BACK!

Mabuhay Gardens

443 Broadway, S.F.

Oct. 20   9:30

the **BLACk WEDGE**
tour

1 step
EASIER   smashing **SEXISM.**
than punk.   We want to set
5 political   some wild hearts and
dynamos.   imaginations free. We want
Hardcore poems   to release a riot of emotion
wild vocals   - opening up a new arena
shredding guitars.   for activist resistance culture.
Radical voices   Disintegrating **CONFORMITY.**
crushing **MILITARISM**   And hey, it's going to be fun too.

JUNE 5

MABUHAY GARDENS

RHYTHM ACTIVISM
Norman Nawrocki: poetry
Dam Stink: guitar

"People are struggling, they want to be free.
They long for the day they'll breathe in liberty.
People want their liberty -
they're dying to be free."
▶ 40 minute debut cassette available now.

Mecca Normal
Jean Smith: lyrics
David Lester: guitar

"Almost worse than the pain in my stomach
is knowing that nobody loves me.
I could live or die. Scares the hell out of me."
▶ LP available now.

driver: Scary Failure

dave pritchett poetry
"They felt the danger, in the news, every damn day.
Get dark.
Get drunk. Go dance."

KEN LESTER poetry
"Are we always going to fall
before the final battle call.
Are we ever going to change?"
▶ Long awaited book out this fall.

BRYAN JAMES words
and music
"Believing everything that's said.
Believing there's peace in war.
Believing there is life when I'm... braindead."

thanks to Kris Carlason

RAGE OF

EDEN

theStone

w/LORDS OF THE NEW CHURCH

NIGHTBREAK

Fri. 9

AUG

SUSHI Sun. 7

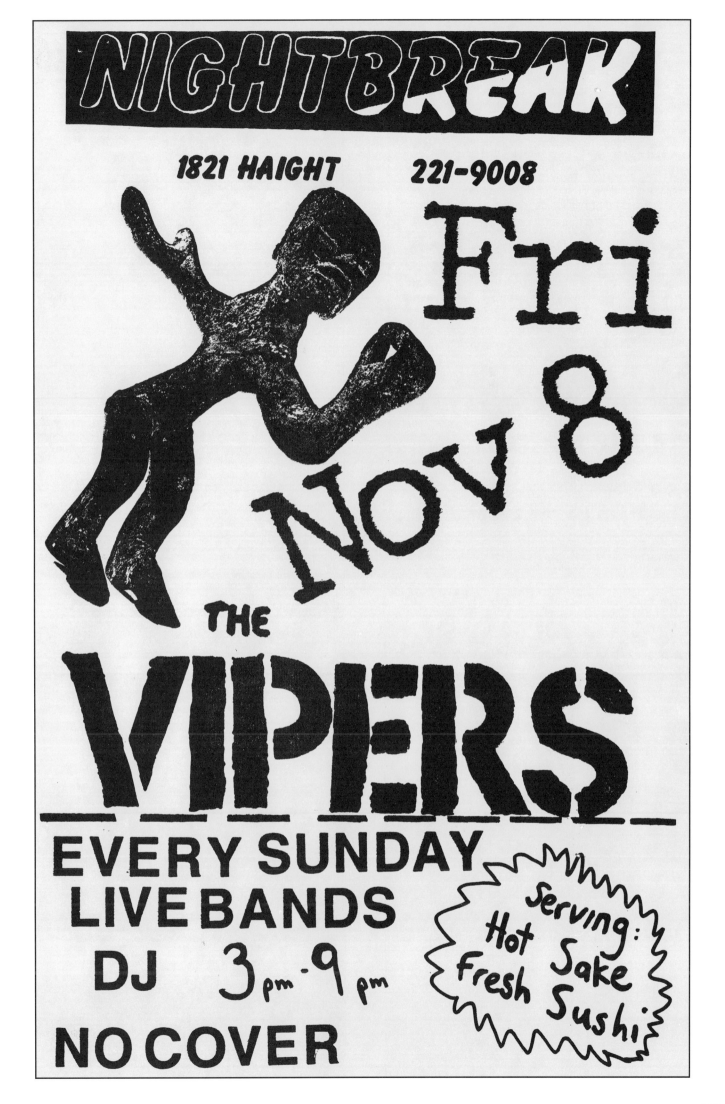

NIGHTBREAK

1821 HAIGHT   221-9008

Fri
Nov 8

THE
VIPERS

EVERY SUNDAY
LIVE BANDS
DJ 3pm-9pm

Serving:
Hot Sake
Fresh Sushi

NO COVER

169

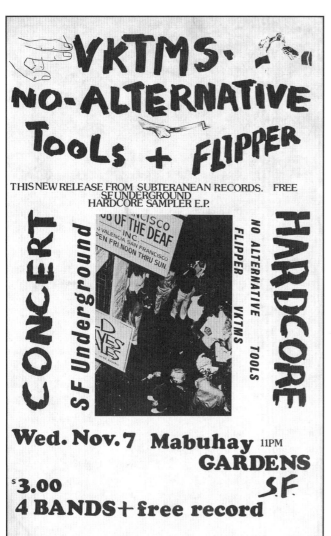

VKTMS.
NO-ALTERNATIVE
TOOLS + FLIPPER

THIS NEW RELEASE FROM SUBTERANEAN RECORDS. FREE SF UNDERGROUND HARDCORE SAMPLER E.P.

CONCERT SF Underground

HARDCORE

FLIPPER NO ALTERNATIVE TOOLS VKTMS

Wed. Nov. 7 Mabuhay 11PM
GARDENS S.F.

$3.00
4 BANDS + free record

Gather Round Oh Beautiful Specimen Mutants

AT The Mab
443 Broadway 956-3315
Saturday May 3
Two Shows
Curfew Show
ALL AGES
6:00 - 10:00
Late Show
10:00 - 2:00

THE BLANK

MABUHAY GARDENS

A DIRKSEN-MILLER PRODUCTION

TICKETS AT ALL B.A.S.S. OUTLETS

"WAR MAY BE HELL, BUT WE LIKE IT"
THURS. JULY 27
11 P.M.
WITH CRIME

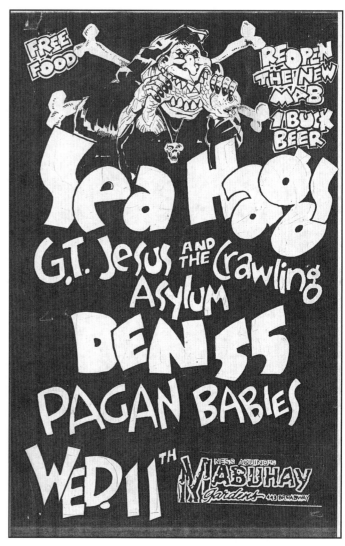

FREE FOOD

REOPEN THE NEW MAB
1 BUCK BEER

Sea Hags
G.T. Jesus AND THE Crawling Asylum
DEN 55
PAGAN BABIES
WED 11TH

NESS AQUINO'S MABUHAY Gardens - 443 Broadway

170

172

NIGHTBREAK

221 9008
1821 Haight St.

Fri Dec 27

AMOK

industrial mix
EVERY SUNDAY 3-9pm

LIVE BANDS

NO COVER
this sunday
DJ SLOVENLY

serving
fresh sushi
hot sake

THE MORLOCKS

WITH
THE
MIRACLE WORKERS
THE SEA HAGS

SAT.   SEPT. 28

BROTHERHOOD OF GM

MC: JERRY CORNELIUS
D.J.: BARRY ST. VITUS (K-ALX)
SWEEDISH-AMERICAN HALL 2174 MARKET ST
9:00 PM   ALL AGES/FULL BAR $5

NIGHTBREAK

our lady of

pain

fri jan 24

221-9008   1821 Haight St

☆ hey every SUNDAY afternoon o.k.   ☆
☆ LIVE BANDS   NO COVER   cool right   ☆
☆ tough D.J.   uh yea 21 over always   ☆
☆ 3 to 9 pm NO COVER TILL 9 food too?   ☆

INDOOR LIFE
ROOSEVELT: March 2 (400), 28
INTERSECTION: 7,8 -14,15 - 21,22
OUTSTANDING IN THEIR FIELD

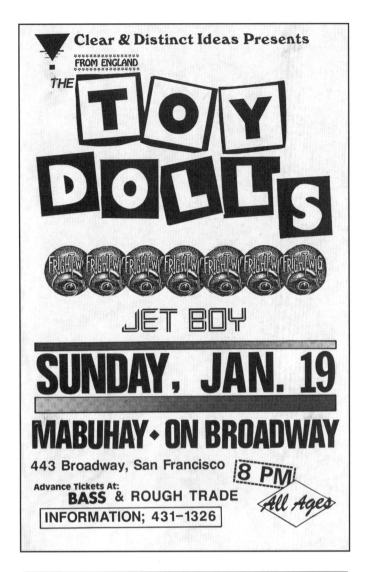

Clear & Distinct Ideas Presents
FROM ENGLAND
THE

TOY DOLLS

FRIGHTWIG FRIGHTWIG FRIGHTWIG FRIGHTWIG FRIGHTWIG FRIGHTWIG FRIGHTWIG

JET BOY

SUNDAY, JAN. 19

MABUHAY ◆ ON BROADWAY

443 Broadway, San Francisco   **8 PM**

Advance Tickets At:
BASS & **ROUGH TRADE**   *All Ages*

INFORMATION; 431-1326

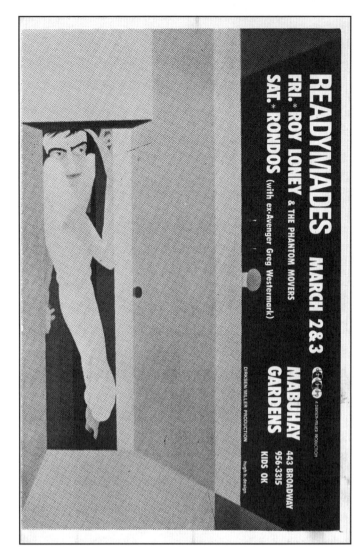

READYMADES
FRI.* ROY LONEY & THE PHANTOM MOVERS
SAT.* RONDOS (with ex-Avenger Greg Westermark)

MARCH 2 & 3

MABUHAY GARDENS

443 BROADWAY
956-3315
KIDS OK

A DIRKSEN-MILLER PRODUCTION

hugh b design

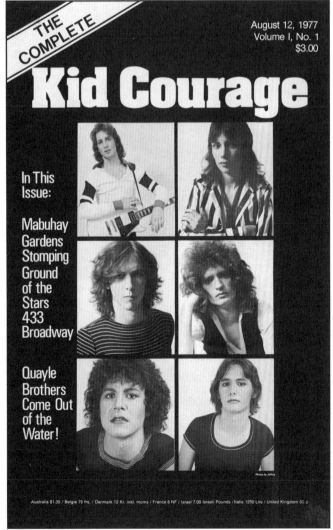

THE COMPLETE

August 12, 1977
Volume I, No. 1
$3.00

Kid Courage

In This
Issue:

Mabuhay
Gardens
Stomping
Ground
of the
Stars
433
Broadway

Quayle
Brothers
Come Out
of the
Water!

Photos by Jeffrey

Australia $1.35 / Belgie 75 frs. / Danmark 12 Kr. inkl. moms / France 8 NF / Israel 7.00 Israeli Pounds / Italia 1250 Lire / United Kingdom 60 p

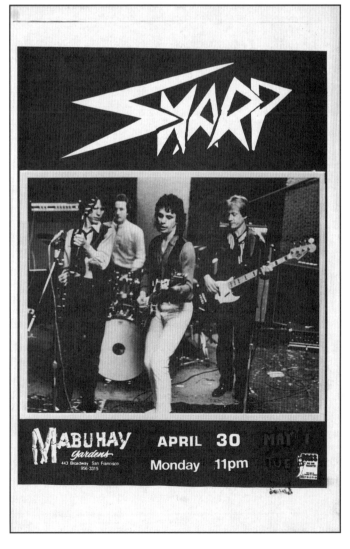

SYDR

MABUHAY
Gardens
443 Broadway San Francisco
956-3315

APRIL 30
Monday   11pm

MAY 1
TUE

SPOT 10 19!!

VIS CLUB

FRI. DEC. 12

628 DIVISADERO

10:19 PM (EARTH TIME)

WITH THIN WHITE ROPE & DENIM T.V.

SLOAN

THU., SEPT. 5

Chi Chi club

440 BROADWAY SF 392-6213

watch for the Speed Queen's EP in Sept.

HENRY KAISER BAND

PLUS SPECIAL GUESTS

LEAVING TRAINS

628 DIVISADERO

SATURDAY,
NOVEMBER 21

DOORS OPEN 9:00
SHOWTIME 10:00
TICKETS AVAILABLE AT
BASS
$7.00 AT THE DOOR

SPOT 1019

VIS
628 DIVISADERO 5670520

APRIL 22

ONLY $2 COVER

75¢ BEERS

WACKY WEDNESDAY!!

OPAL

Groovin' in the sky with Jackets

$6 at the door

w/ DOWNEY MILDEW

FRI, JULY 8

KENNEL CLUB
628 DIVISADERO

VAIN

AT THE STONE

FRI. MARCH 4th

DOORS OPEN 8:00

WITH THE **

SEA HAGS

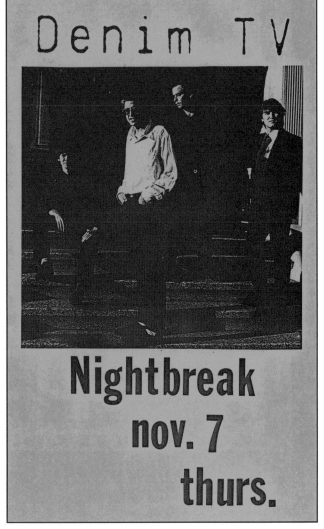

Denim TV

Nightbreak
nov. 7
thurs.

178

KUSF/KALX CO-PRESENT A BAY AREA EXCLUSIVE
MONDAY APRIL 20
fIREHOSE
SAQQARA DOGS
DC3

I-BEAM
1748 HAIGHT ST.
ADVANCE TIX AT I-BEAM, REVOLVER, HALL OF RECORDS
ROUGH TRADE, RECKLESS, AQUARIUS, DALJEETS & BASS
MONDAY APRIL 27: MOTÖRHEAD

180

MONDAY JAN.18
fIREHOSE
SCREAMING TREES

I BEAM

KUSF/KALX
CO·PRESENT
A BAY AREA
EXCLUSIVE

1748 HAIGHT ST.
ADVANCE TIX AT I-BEAM
REVOLVER, AQUARIUS
ROUGH TRADE, RECKLESS
HALL OF RECORDS & BASS

MON. JULY 29

KUSF/BAM/KALX CO-PRESENT A BAY AREA EXCLUSIVE

DIAMANDA GALAS

NAZIM OZEL
AND HIS SEMI-CIVILIZED TREE

ADVANCE TIX AT I BEAM
ROUGH TRADE, AQUARIUS,
REVOLVER, & DALJEET'S

I BEAM

AUG 5 - GREEN ON RED
FLAMING LIPS

1748 HAIGHT ST

MON JUNE 10

KUSF/BAM/KALX CO-PRESENT

BAY AREA EXCLUSIVE

THE KNITTERS

FROM L.A.

the Washington Squares

FROM N.Y.C.

JUNE 17 - BEAT FARMERS

JUNE 24 - ROBYN HITCHCOCK/ALEX CHILTON

I BEAM

1748 HAIGHT ST

MURMURS

rock & roll

fullmoon

murmurs.

After the Fireworks, The Fire STILL BURNS.

!

1725 HAiGHT

(ANGELS WiTH DiRTY GUiTARS)

THE FULL MOON saloon

JULY 4th

-WITH *
The ArT OFFiCiALS

184

DEAD MARILYN

BACK BY POPULAR DEMAND!
SEE REVENGE THRU THE
EYES OF A DEAD WOMAN
KENNEL CLUB SAT. 26 SEPT. 6$

087506
ADMIT ONE
Pray For Rain
IMPULSE F
boxing factory
Formerly PARIS WORKING
087506
at SAT. DECEMBER 7
VIS CLUB
628 DIVISADERO
DOORS OPEN 9:00 $5

NIGHTBREAK
SHIVA DANCING
SHE DEVILS
MAGIC OF SITAR
featuring RAM
SATURDAY, APRIL 9
SPEEDWAY RECORDS

sat 24
maximillions'
M.C.
NIGHTBREAK
1821 Haight 221-9008

MONDAY APRIL 11

KUSF / KALX / KFJC CO-PRESENT

⊕ THE ⊕
GUN CLUB
FRONTIER WIVES

ADVANCE TIX AT I-BEAM
REVOLVER, HALL OF RECORDS
ROUGH TRADE, RECKLESS
AQUARIUS & BASS

1748 HAIGHT ST. [at COLE] ⊕ ADVANCE TIX $8 ⊕ DOOR $9

TR

BAY AREA EXCLUSIVE

THE UNDERWORLD

FROM THE UK

FRIDAY JUNE 3

DOORS OPEN 9

SHOW TIME 10

SPECIAL GUESTS

KENNEL CLUB
628 DIVISADERO

$6/7 AVAILABLE AT BASS

SISTER DOUBLE HAPINESS
LAWN VULTURES

KENNEL CLUB
628 DIVISADERO

FRIDAY DEC. 18
DOORS OPEN 9:00
SHOWTIME 10:00
$5.00 AT THE DOOR
TICKETS AVAILABLE AT
BASS

NIGHTBREAK
FRIDAY Sept. 30th

DAS DAMEN

& SHORT DOGS GROW
Door 9pm

SPEEDWAY RECORDS

NIGHTBreaK
1821 Haight 221-9008

BUZZ IN THE SYSTEM
AND ALSO:
JOHNNY RAVEN

WED. June 22nd

SPEEDWAY RECORDS

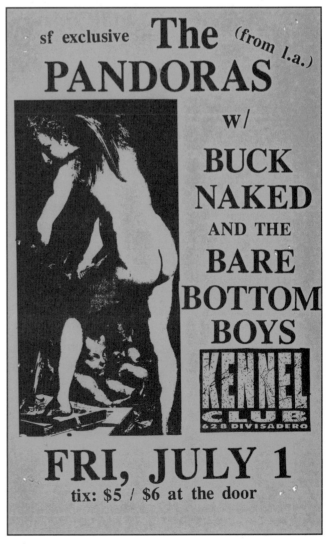

sf exclusive The (from l.a.)
PANDORAS
w/
BUCK NAKED
AND THE
BARE
BOTTOM
BOYS

KENNEL CLUB
628 DIVISADERO

FRI, JULY 1
tix: $5 / $6 at the door

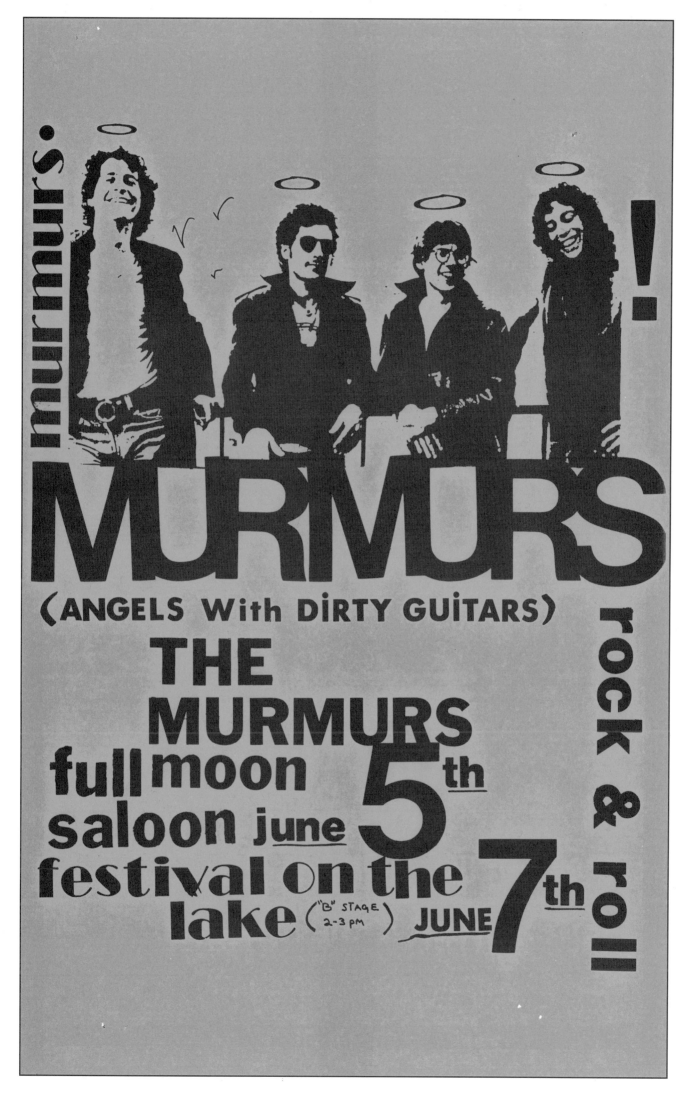

189

190

THE STONE
SAT. JULY 20

WITH

VOICE FARM

A PRIVATE VIEW

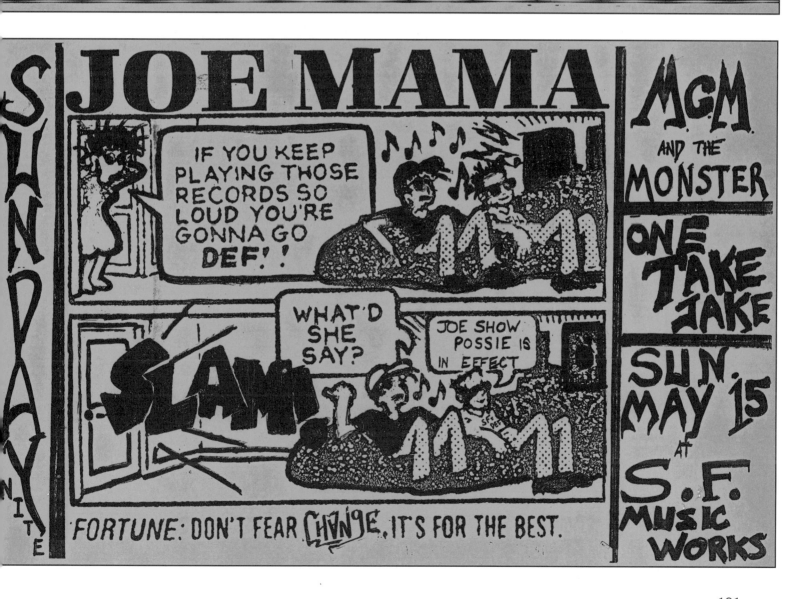

New Year's Eve Dance Party!

The City 98.9 Fm WELCOMES

STEVIE RAY VAUGHAN AND DOUBLE TROUBLE

PLUS SPECIAL GUESTS

TOWER OF POWER

JR. WALKER AND THE ALL STARS

THE PALADINS

**NEW YEAR'S EVE • THURSDAY, DECEMBER 31, 8PM
HENRY J. KAISER CONVENTION CENTER, OAKLAND**

193

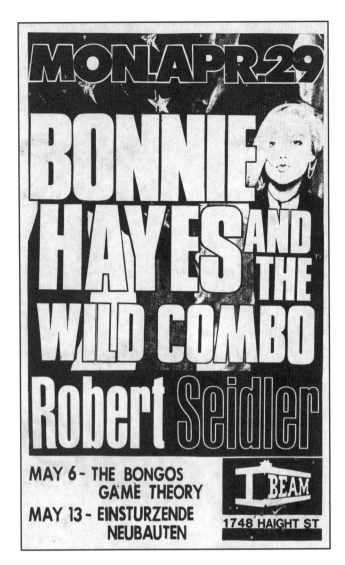

MON. APR. 29

BONNIE HAYES AND THE WILD COMBO

Robert Seidler

MAY 6 - THE BONGOS
GAME THEORY

MAY 13 - EINSTURZENDE
NEUBAUTEN

I BEAM

1748 HAIGHT ST

NIGHTBREAK
1821 Haight 221-9008

Sat. July 9

HOUSE OF WHEELS

AND

THE BIRDKILLERS

DOOR 9pm 4 $

SPEEDWAY RECORDS

NIGHTBREAK

OH, M'GAWD!

BLACKBIRD
featuring Chip & Tony of "Rank & File" fame

+ Special guests:

MCM and the MONSTER

DYNAMITE BIRDSEED

FRI., MAY 27th

SPEEDWAY RECORDS

MON. MAR. 18
KUSF/BAM/KALX CO-PRESENT FROM THE U.K.

RED LORRY YELLOW LORRY

CRAWL AWAY MACHINE

ADVANCE TIX AT ROUGH
TRADE, DISTRACTIONS,
REVOLVER, DALJEET'S
AQUARIUS & I BEAM

MAR. 25, 26 - THE FALL

I BEAM

1748 HAIGHT ST

LAST DATE BEFORE NATIONAL TOUR

YANKS

FRIDAY FEB. 1

AT THE

ROCK ON

WITH EXPATRIOTS AND MODERN VOICES

BROADWAY

HALLOWEEN
AT THE KENNEL CLUB

JANE'S ADDICTION
(FROM L.A.)

SEA HAGS

KENNEL
CLUB
628 DIVISADERO

SATURDAY, OCTOBER 31
10:00 SHARP $8.00

SATURDAY 9 JANUARY

SURF OR DIE

SURF MC'S

SURF
SKATE
RELATE

NIGHTBREAK

SHOW STARTS 11:30

TIX 6$

197

DANCE

I BEAM

THURSDAYS ▪ D.J. BRIAN RAFFI
STUDENTS FREE

FRIDAYS ▪ D.J. NEON LEON
STUDENTS $2 OFF

1748 HAIGHT ST. (AT COLE)

MONDAY MAY 11
KUSF/KALX CO-PRESENT
THE LORRIES
GT JESUS and the CRAWLING ASYLUM

1748 HAIGHT ST. I BEAM

ADVANCE TIX AT I-BEAM, REVOLVER, HALL OF RECORDS
ROUGH TRADE, RECKLESS, AQUARIUS, DALJEETS & BASS
MONDAY MAY 18 : REDD KROSS ● THE GODFATHERS

crawl away machine

NIGHT BREAK
Friday the 16th
10:00 pm

NIGHTBreak
1821 Haight 221-9008

FRIDAY
July 1
BEATNIGS
two sets

...door 9pm $4/5
SPEEDWAY RECORDS

MONDAY NOV. 2
KUSF/KALX CO-PRESENT A BAY AREA EXCLUSIVE
CRAZY BACKWARDS ALPHABET
JOHN FRENCH ● HENRY KAISER ● ANDY WEST
OGIE YOCHA

I BEAM

1748 HAIGHT ST.
ADVANCE TIX AT I-BEAM, REVOLVER, ROUGH TRADE
HALL OF RECORDS, RECKLESS, AQUARIUS & BASS

RETRO-DELIC

AN **ATA**
ARTIST & TELEVISION ACCESS

featuring
THE DWARVES
CAROLINER RAINBOW
and a Webwear
Walk-on

BENEFIT
BE-IN

ADM $5

Thurs June 18th 8-12pm then disco with
375
11th at the **DNA lounge**
street

DJ Ted Cousins

IMPULSE F

Z AXIS

BAYBRICK

552-1121

Wednesday
November 6
9 PM $5

AMC
last show of 1985

Desire

HOUSECOAT
V. PROJECT
I. S.
628 Divisadero

friday june 7

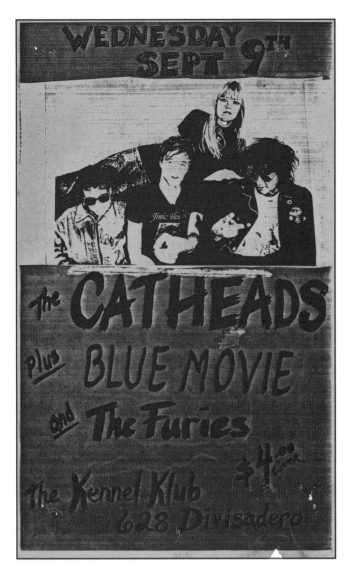

WEDNESDAY
SEPT 9TH

The CATHEADS
plus BLUE MOVIE
and The Furies
$4.00 each
The Kennel Klub
628 Divisadero

Jeffrey Normal & MAGICK
Return to Normalcy

THE STONE
NOV. 27TH

4/21
THVRS Das Damen
SLOVENLY
DRUNK
Edgy Marines Being Probed INJUNS
Beneath A Vast 'Lake' in Panama

SAN FRANCISCO
MUSIC WORKS

Tragical
History
Tour 10 PM

"Wild Animals March to Palmetto State" *m.85*

↓ Mabuhay Gardens Thursday August 22

↓ The 16th Note Sunday August 25

Palmetto State

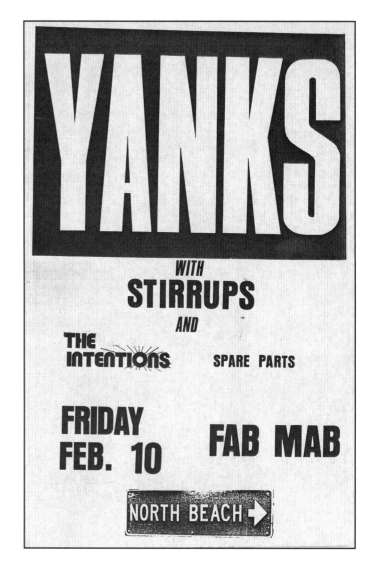

YANKS

WITH **STIRRUPS**

AND

THE INTENTIONS   SPARE PARTS

FRIDAY FEB. 10   **FAB MAB**

NORTH BEACH →

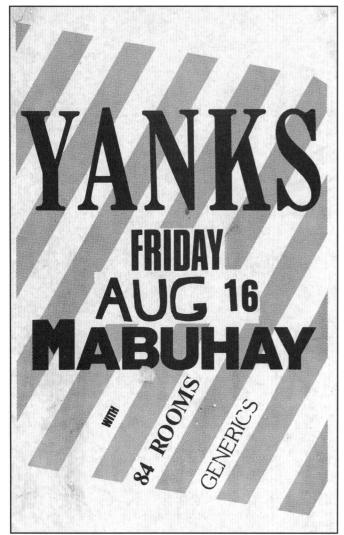

YANKS

FRIDAY AUG 16

MABUHAY

WITH 84 ROOMS   GENERICS

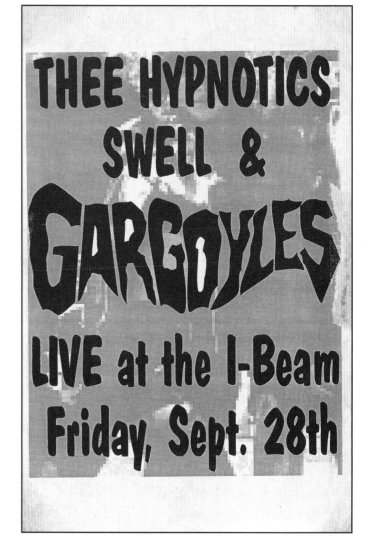

THEE HYPNOTICS SWELL & GARGOYLES

LIVE at the I-Beam Friday, Sept. 28th

Palmetto State
Thursday May 9
Mabuhay Gardens
Also: Denim TV, Non Fiction and DiFi

Nü Lang gwei

MABUHAY ON BROADWAY
SATURDAY AUGUST 10TH 9pm
WITH STICK FIGURES AND ENFORCER
TIX: 415/459-6893
$5 advance $6 nite of show

the children's hour
AT THE MAB

sept. 16th
for more info: 956-3315

BLACK DOLLS
FIRE MISSION
MABUHAY GARDENS
Dirt Tribe
FRY JULY 5th

204

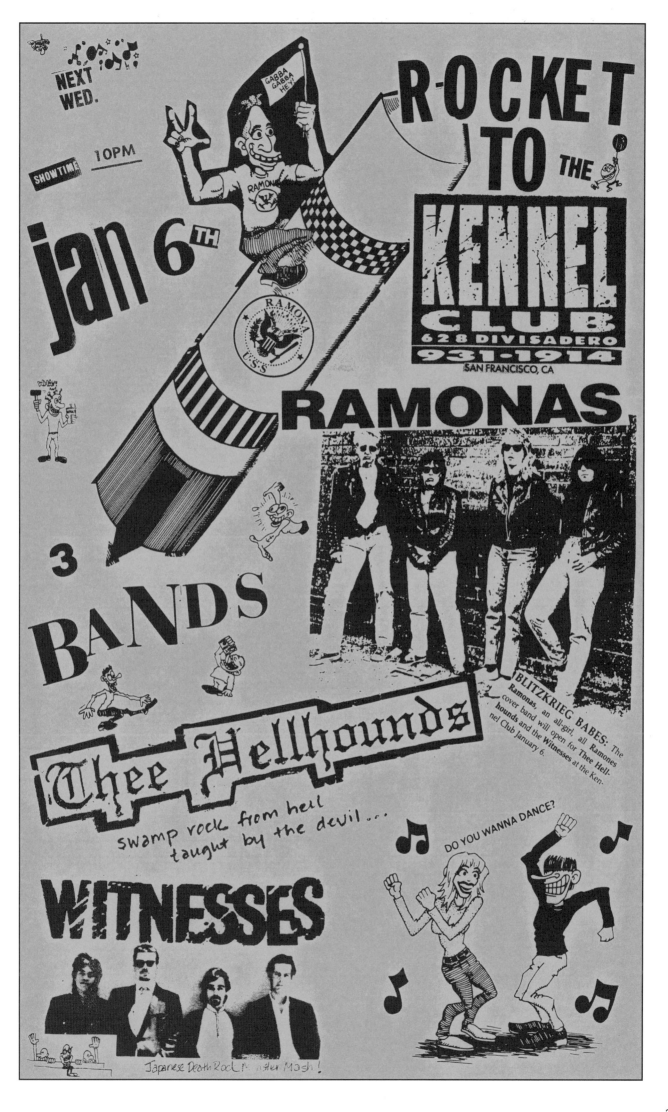

NEXT WED.

SHOWTIME 10PM

GABBA GABBA HEY!

JAN 6TH

ROCKET TO THE KENNEL CLUB
628 DIVISADERO
931-1914
SAN FRANCISCO, CA

RAMONAS

3 BANDS

Thee Hellhounds

swamp rock from hell
taught by the devil...

BLITZKRIEG BABES: The Ramonas, an all-girl, all Ramones cover band will open for Thee Hellhounds and the Witnesses at the Kennel Club January 6.

WITNESSES

Japanese Death Rock Monster Mash!

DO YOU WANNA DANCE?

CONTRACTIONS
(send off for East Coast tour)

and the
Saints

Cover: $2

SEPTEMBER 22

at the

I-BEAM

1748 Haight (at Cole)

Video: Ted Ladd & Co.
Disks: Alan Robinson

S.M.E.G.M.A.

Photo: Jack Dart

sub rosa

Sat 25 July 11 PM

MABUHAY GARDENS

443 BROADWAY, S.F.

SAT. SEPT. 13

tav falco's

PANTHER BURNS

and

Love 'Em Or Hate 'Em

BOSS HOSS

BAY AREA EXCLUSIVE

956-3315

MABUHAY 443 BROADWAY

MON. JULY 15

Battle of the Garage Bands!

psych-out '85!!

THE VIPERS FROM N.Y.

THE **LEAVING TRAINS** FROM L.A.

DOORS OPEN AT 9PM

SHOWTIME AT 10PM

AND **BOSS HOSS** FROM FRISCO

YO MAMA

I BEAM

1748 HAIGHT ST

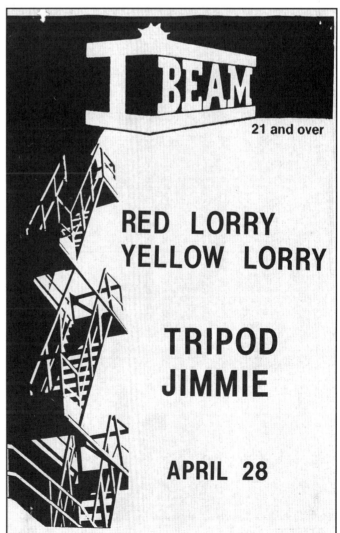

I BEAM

21 and over

RED LORRY YELLOW LORRY

TRIPOD JIMMIE

APRIL 28

HALLOWEEN
MASQUERADE PARTY
COLLEGE OF MARIN

ALLIES

FARALLON

with special guest
TIMMY

general 3.00
students 2.50
tickets available through BASS
and evening of show

FREE TO ASCOM CARD HOLDERS

FRIDAY, OCTOBER 31
COLLEGE CENTER   8:00 p.m.

ASCOM / REMOTE PROMOTION
further info. - 456-4071

⊗WATERBABY

Saturday Night

JULY 16

LET'S ROCK THIS PLACE!

ROSE & THISTLE

1624 CALIFORNIA ~ at Polk $1 Cover

JAI JAI NOIRE
& THE ORIGINAL BEASTS
AND
TYPHOON

NOV. 11

HARD ROCK DANCING
W/THE D.J. KIM DANDERS

Rockers!

WEDNESDAY 9-2
6TH & HARRISON (ENDUP)
FREE ADMISSION/$1 BEER
BEFORE 10PM

PLENTY OF FREE PARKING
$1 BOTTLE BEER
BEFORE 10PM

IN PRAISE OF OUTLAWS

photo by mary skram

GLORIOUS DIN

BARNACLE CHOIR
FROM SANTA CRUZ
WINNEBAGO BROS
FROM L.A
WORLD OF POOH

FILMS 8 30
SWISS AMERICAN HALL
2174 MARKET ST

SAT 17 AUG

MINORS WELCOME

mary
Monday

at the famous
Palms oct 17th

211

DNA LOUNGE **IN CONCERT**

SEAHAGS

Earth Panorama: Africa 2

WED. JULY 29

RECORD CONTRACT SIGNING PARTY

9 PM $5.00

Followed By "COLD SWEAT"
Dancing with Dj Adam Fisher
Midnight to 4 AM

21 & OLDER   PLEASE HAVE I.D.
375 11th Street   626-1409

RHYTHM PIGS
C.TOWN ALLEY
RABID LASSIE
KILL
SAT. JAN 18
CLUBFOOT
2520 3rd St.
8Pm $4

FOLK ART INTERNATIONAL

The maids

TUES.
NOV.
25

16th
NOTE

Caesar Buonarroti

AT 16th/Valencia

SALE—FOR CHRISTMAS
NOV. 22-DEC. 28—FORT MASON
CONFERENCE CENTER (BLDG. A), SAN FRANCISCO
TUES.-SAT. 10AM-8PM, SUN. & MON. 10AM-6PM
JEWELRY, MASKS, TOYS, BASKETS, CLOTHING,
SCULPTURE, FABRICS AND DECORATIONS FROM:
PAPUA NEW GUINEA, JAPAN, CHINA, SOUTHEAST ASIA,
AFRICA, EUROPE, MEXICO, NORTH AND SOUTH AMERICA

UNDERGROUND! "I.D."
PARTY APRIL 14
9 pm. 3 bucks
2001 9th Street
(corner of 9th & Howard)
INFO: 431-1326
I CAN'T WAIT
HOUSE AHEAD -with-

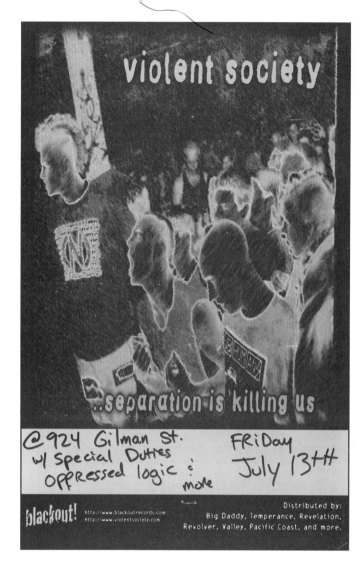

GRAND REOPENING
PUNTS
TARGET VIDEO
SEE SPOT
SAVOY TIVOLY
SUNDAY MARCH 23
4 to 7 PM

VANILLA WHORES
WIG TORTURE CAMELTOE
AT MORTY'S
1024 KEARNY S.F. 18 AND OVER
FRI. SEP. 28 9:00 5$

SEA·HAGS
MORLOCKS
SAT AUG 3
SWEDISH/
AMERICAN·HALL
MARKET & SANCHEZ STREETS

Pointillism
YEASTIE GIRLS
TENDA TEE
DJ'S LEWIS AND MICHAEL
4 NON BLONDS
BOY WITH ARMS AKIMBO
$5 DONATION
AN ACT-UP BENEFIT
FOR PREVENTION POINT
8PM DAS KLUB WED. JAN. 24
1015 FOLSOM STREET

214

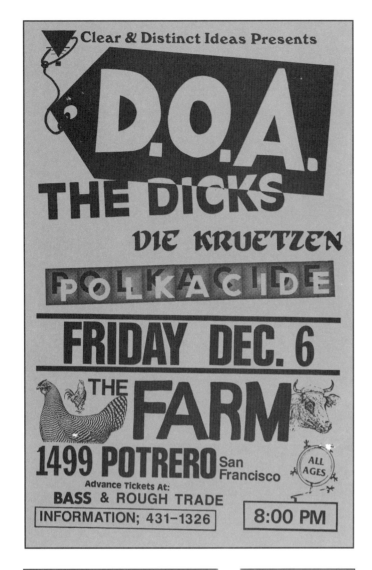

Clear & Distinct Ideas Presents

D.O.A.
THE DICKS
DIE KRUETZEN
POLKACIDE

FRIDAY DEC. 6

THE FARM

1499 POTRERO San Francisco

Advance Tickets At:
BASS & ROUGH TRADE

ALL AGES

INFORMATION; 431-1326

8:00 PM

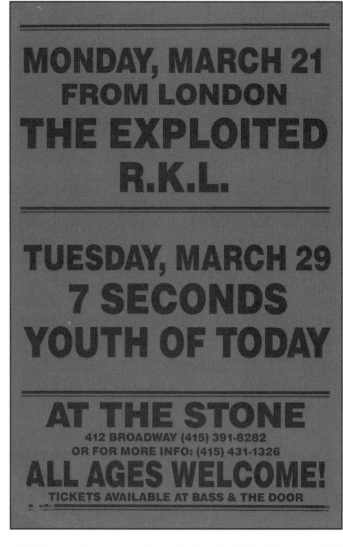

MONDAY, MARCH 21
FROM LONDON
THE EXPLOITED
R.K.L.

TUESDAY, MARCH 29
7 SECONDS
YOUTH OF TODAY

AT THE STONE
412 BROADWAY (415) 391-8282
OR FOR MORE INFO: (415) 431-1326
ALL AGES WELCOME!
TICKETS AVAILABLE AT BASS & THE DOOR

KICK OFF A WILD, WILD SUMMER!

sunday june 4th 1989

the
SNEETCHES
milo binder
SPECIAL GUEST DOUG ORTON & THE LOUISE IN PARIS REVIEW
doors open at 8 show at 9 $3 admission

SUNDAY JUNE 11TH

G.I. JESUS
& the crawling asylum
with special guests
serpent i.d.

doors open at 8 show at 9 $3 admission

THE DNA LOUNGE
375 11th street 626-1409

The San Jose Peace Center
proudly presents
PETE SEEGER
THIS SPECIAL SOLO PERFORMANCE IS A BENEFIT FOR
THE SAN JOSE PEACE CENTER

November 24
Sunday, 2 pm

San Jose Center for the Performing Arts
255 Almaden at Park, San Jose

TICKETS ARE:
$30 patron
$12.50 general
All seats are reserved.
Wheelchair access is available.
Please call ahead at
408-297-2299 or **408-297-6660**

Tickets are available through all BASS outlets
including Record Factory Stores.
To charge by phone, call:

408 998-2277 or 998-BASS
415 762-2277 or 762-BASS

Tickets may also be purchased directly by sending
a self-addressed, stamped envelope to:

THE SAN JOSE PEACE CENTER
PETE SEEGER CONCERT
478 W. HAMILTON, SUITE 303
CAMPBELL, CA 95008

Make checks payable to: San Jose Peace Center/
Pete Seeger Concert

A special reception will be held following the
concert. Tickets are $20 and space is limited.
Order through the Peace Center Address above.

Gala Masquerade Ball

The UNREAL BAND

FRIDAY EVE

OCTOBER 31

MASTER OF CEREMONIES
WAVY GRAVY

9:30 PM $5.00 AT THE DOOR

FACE PAINTING AND MONSTER MAKE-UP WILL
BE AVAILABLE FOR A SMALL FEE
COSTUME CONTEST! GRAND PRIZE: 25 CLAMS!

ASHKENAZ
1370 San Pablo Ave. Berkeley

Halloween Extravaganza

©1986 Thos Chapman

217

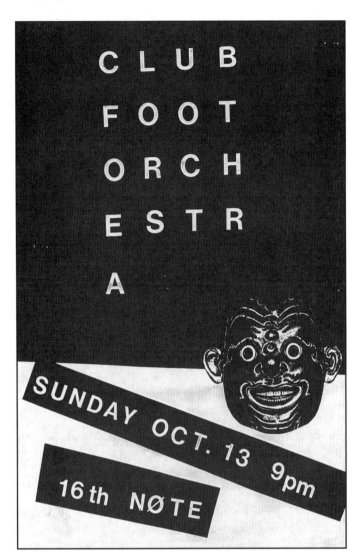

CLUB
FOOT
ORCH
ESTR
A

SUNDAY OCT. 13   9pm

16 th NØTE

TOO
MUCH
FUN
FRI·JAN·31
16 NOTE
3160 16th ST.

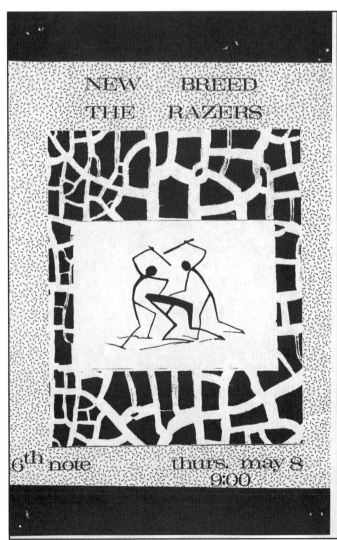

NEW   BREED
THE   RAZERS

6th note   thurs. may 8
9:00

THE RAZERS

JULY 24
THUrs.
16th note
10 pm

JULY 25
friday
the mabuhay
9 pm

TUESDAY OCT. 13 9PM
CAROLINER RAINBOW
ARCHIPELAGO BREWING CO.

LIPPS UNDERGROUND
9TH AND HOWARD

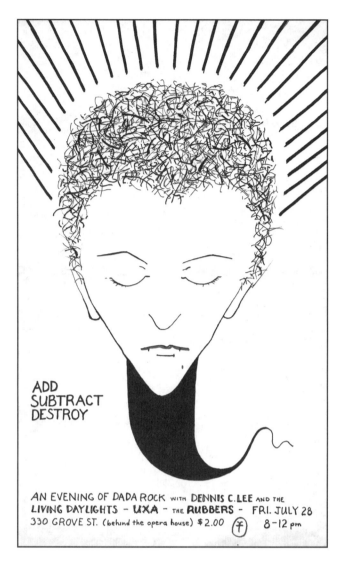

ADD
SUBTRACT
DESTROY

AN EVENING OF DADA ROCK WITH DENNIS C. LEE AND THE
LIVING DAYLIGHTS - UXA - THE RUBBERS - FRI. JULY 28
330 GROVE ST. (behind the opera house) $2.00 (f) 8-12 pm

eryrhing is special at
club CONFIDENTIAL
SEMETARY
Fri. SEPT 6

FOR FAST
PICK-UP

At:
FACES FACES
1550 CALIFORNIA

$5.00 At the Door
$4.00 With Invite

ID please
(21 & OVER)

BOSS
HOSS

WITH CRITICAL CHIP
SAT. MAY 25
HOTEL UTAH

AT THE
CRYSTAL PISTOL
BACK STAGE!
21 & over only!!
THE SUNDAY MAY 1st: 3:00 PM
ADOLESCENTS FROM LA!
842 VALENCIA St. ONLY $3 bucks!
BETWEEN 19th AND 20th St. ACROSS FROM the CHATTERBOX.

ALSO ON MAY 7th
INFORMATION 431-1326
FRONTLINE FROM S.J.
AND MYSTERIE TRAIN A RAMPAGE PRODUCTION
ROCK OUT!

Defectors
FRIDAY
Sept.
13
Faces
Faces

1550 Calif. St. NEAR POLK

Defectors
SUN.
JULY
14th
4:00
in the afternoon
san
francisco
art
on the roof.
institute.

800 chestnut st. S.F.

ROCK HARD ATTRACTIONS
proudly presents:

Photo: MARK WEISS

MADAM X
Plus very special guests

DOLL
SHOCK THE WORLD

SAN FRANCISCO'S GLAM KINGS
JETBOY

THE
ROXY
THEATRE
SUNDAY, JUNE 9th

FOR INFO CALL: (818) 785-3785   DOORS OPEN AT 7:30 P.M.

ALL FRINGE!
WELCOME
SAT. NOON   HAIGHT / COLE   SAT. NOON

SQUAT LOT
SiR 'X' ART

TUESDAY DECEMBER 8 9PM
IOWA TANK
WORLD OF POOH
LIPPS UNDERGROUND
9TH AND HOWARD

853 valencia
CHATTERBOX
THE RETURN OF
BOSS HOSS
RAMONAS
FRI.
Nov. 20

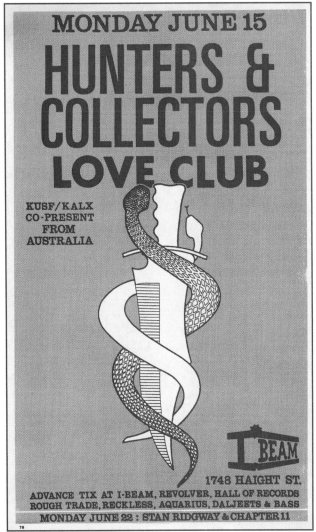

MONDAY JUNE 15
**HUNTERS &
COLLECTORS**
LOVE CLUB
KUSF/KALX
CO-PRESENT
FROM
AUSTRALIA
I-BEAM
1748 HAIGHT ST.
ADVANCE TIX AT I-BEAM, REVOLVER, HALL OF RECORDS
ROUGH TRADE, RECKLESS, AQUARIUS, DALJEETS & BASS
MONDAY JUNE 22 : STAN RIDGWAY & CHAPTER 11

KUSF/KALX
CO-PRESENT A SF EXCLUSIVE
MONDAY NOV. 9
DUMPTRUCK
HOUSE OF FREAKS
THE SNEETCHES
$5
I-BEAM
1748 HAIGHT ST.

jongon with BIRD BRAIN PARTY visit & EYES OF MARCH at the MARUHAY

SATURDAY NOVEMBER 16

NIGHTBREAK
sat., june 18th
the CRAZY 8'S
SPEEDWAY RECORDS

It's just another year you've drowned
CRIS LOITER & THE HANGOUTS
help us Celebrate! our first Anniversary
SATURDAY DECEMBER 7th
THE STONE

SHIVA DANCING
and
Sister Double Happiness
Thursday 7/30
628 Divisadero st.
931-1914
KENNEL CLUB

SEE THE
METAL BROTHERS
the best   the best   The Best
the best   THE BEST
THE BEST   the best
the BEST!
THRASH
METAL BAND
in the
South BAY
POSERS
at The STONE
412 broadway S.F.
WED NOVEMBER 13   8 o'clock PM
ADVANCED tickets $4.00

MON SEPT. 30

KUSF / KALX CO-PRESENT
A BAY AREA EXCLUSIVE
FROM THE U.K.

the lucy show

OCT 7 -
POISON GIRLS
BEAT RODEO

MRS. GREEN

I-BEAM
1748 HAIGHT ST

MONDAY AUGUST 12
NECROPOLIS OF LOVE

AUG 19 - THE
LOOTERS
AUG 26 - THE
FLESHTONES

UNTIL DECEMBER

I-BEAM
1748 HAIGHT ST

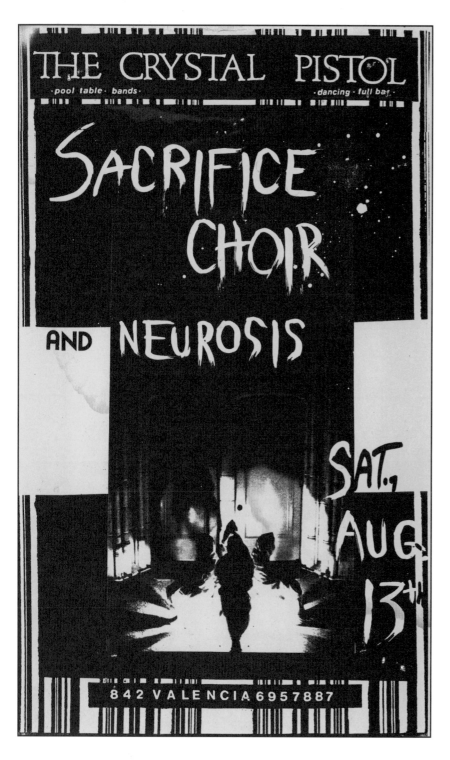

THE CRYSTAL PISTOL
· pool table · bands ·   · dancing · full bar

SACRIFICE
CHOIR
AND NEUROSIS

SAT.,
AUG.
13th

842 VALENCIA 6957887

GET YOUR MONKEYS OUT WITH

JETBOY

KIX

ALL AGES
7 pm

FRI   DECEMBER 6th ON BROADWAY

Lazy
Sunday
Dreamers

Chatterbox
853
Valencia

Oct. 17
10pm
Friday

228

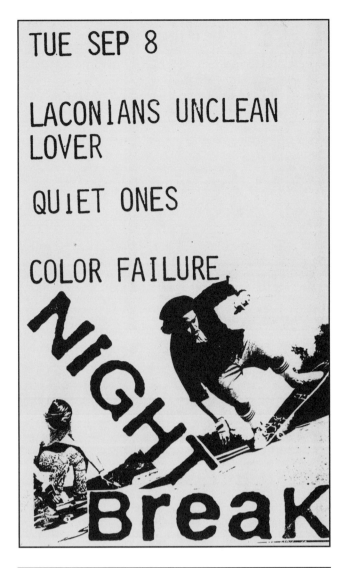

TUE SEP 8

LACONIANS UNCLEAN
LOVER

QUIET ONES

COLOR FAILURE

NIGHT
Break

CRAZY 8s

also SQUARE ROOTS

KENNEL CLUB
628 DIVISADERO

SAT.
MAR. 19

DOORS OPEN 9:00
SHOWTIME 10:30
$6.00 IN ADVANCE
$7.00 DAY OF SHOW
TICKETS AVAILABLE
AT BASS

RAIN PARADE

MISSILE HARMONY
FRI 24 JUNE $6

KENNEL CLUB
628 DIVISADERO

doors open
9:00
showtime
10:00

NIGHT
BREAK

THIS SUN.
AUG 3
SYMPHONY
OF SATIRE

NO
GRENADES
4PM

SUSHI

☆ hey every SUNDAY afternoon o.k. ☆
☆ LIVE BANDS   NO COVER   cool   ☆
☆ tough D.J. uh yea 21 over   ☆
☆ 3 to 9 pm NO COVER TILL 9   ☆

TUESDAY, MARCH 29
7 SECONDS
YOUTH OF TODAY

AT THE STONE
412 BROADWAY (415) 391-8282
OR FOR MORE INFO: (415) 431-1326
ALL AGES WELCOME!
TICKETS AVAILABLE AT BASS & THE DOOR

LIPPS·UNDERGROUND·
IN ASSOCIATION WITH
WARREN SANFØRD/TDL.
PRESENT

sub·cul·ture

201 9th st ‹at Howard› San Fransisco
TUESDAYS

MADE IN THE STATES

YANKS

Paul Zahl   Jack Johnson   Owen Masterson   Steve Aliment

APPEARING AT WOLFGANG'S

FRIDAY FEB. 3

SUPPORTING **ERIC MARTIN BAND**

WITH **ALLEY OPERA**

Neo-Psychedelic
weekend
at
THE FARM
1499 Potrero
826-4290
Friday June 20th
• CAMPER VAN Beethoven
• CAT HEADS
• Blue Movie
• SPOT 1019
Saturday June 21st
• FAITH NO MORE
• U-MEN
• SEA HAGS
• TOUCH ME Hooker
8 pm $7
Lights by
Brotherhood of light

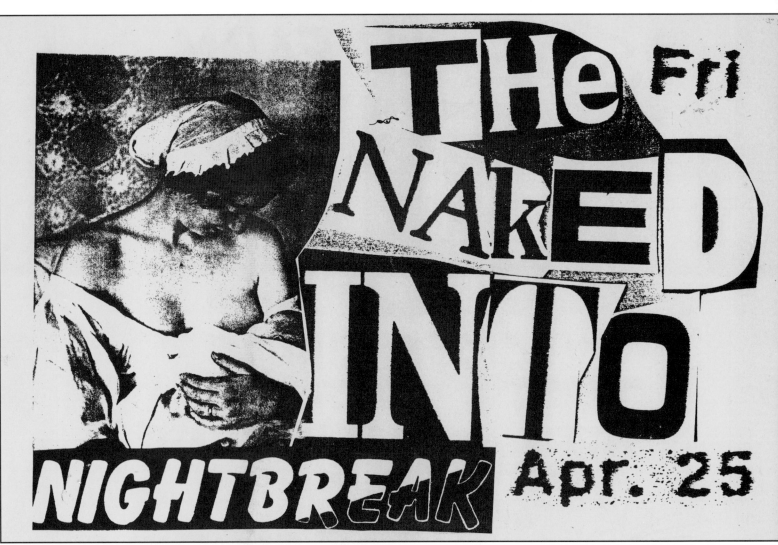

THe Fri
NAKED INTO
NIGHTBREAK Apr. 25

JET boY
june 6
NIGHTBREAK

Clean and jerk. 1950s

FROM ENGLAND
THE EXCLUSIVE BAY AREA APPEARANCE OF

DURAN
DURAN

WITH QUIET ROOM

ADVANCE TICKETS AT B.A.S.S. AND I·BEAM BOX OFFICE

OCT. 5
I~BEAM

MONDAY

1748 HAIGHT
DJ·ALAN
ROBINSON

MON. & TUES. OCT. 20-21

KUSF/KALX Co-Announce — BAY AREA EXCLUSIVE

THE FALL.
LAWNDALE
(MONDAY ONLY)

ADVANCE TIX AT I BEAM
ROUGH TRADE, RECKLESS
REVOLVER, AQUARIUS
& DALJEETS

I BEAM
1748 HAIGHT ST

TUES. OCT. 28 - NICK CAVE

NIGHTBREAK

the Monikers

thurs jan 23

Barking Spiders

☆ ☆ ☆ ☆
hey every SUNDAY afternoon o.k.
LIVE BANDS   NO COVER   cool right
tough D.J.   uh yea   21 over always
3 to 9 pm   NO COVER TILL 9   food too?
☆ ☆ ☆ ☆

1821 Haight 221-9008

NIGHTBREAK
1821 Haight St
221-9008

Thurs Nov 28

TEKNO FEAR

EVERY SUNDAY
LIVE BANDS
DJ 3pm-9pm
NO COVER

Serving:
Hot Sake
Fresh Sushi

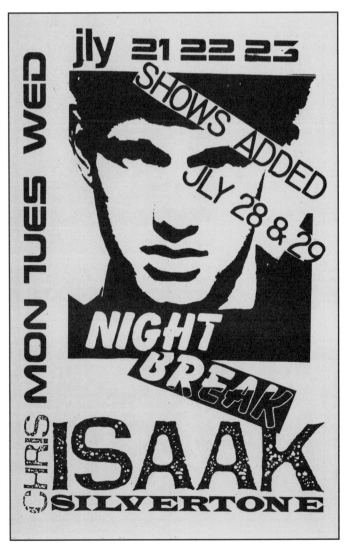

jly 21 22 23

SHOWS ADDED JLY 28 & 29

MON TUES WED

NIGHT BREAK

CHRIS **ISAAK**
SILVERTONE

236

KUSF/KALX CO-PRESENT A BAY AREA EXCLUSIVE

MONDAY APRIL 13

SKINNY PUPPY
EDWARD KA-SPEL
(LEGENDARY PINK DOTS)

I BEAM

1748 HAIGHT ST.

ADVANCE TIX AT I-BEAM, REVOLVER, HALL OF RECORDS
ROUGH TRADE, RECKLESS, AQUARIUS, DALJEETS & BASS
MONDAY APRIL 20: fIREHOSE ● SAQQARA DOGS

WIRE TRAIN
BOHEMIAN LUV JONES

KENNEL CLUB
628 DIVISADERO

FRIDAY, NOVEMBER 27

DOORS OPEN 9:00
SHOWTIME 10:00
TICKETS AVAILABLE AT BASS
$7.00 AT THE DOOR

MON. SEPT. 15
KUSF/KALX CO-ANNOUNCE

Polkacide

CLUB FOOT orchestra

SEPT. 22
RED HOT CHILI PEPPERS
SEPT. 29
GENE LOVES JEZEBEL

I BEAM
1748 HAIGHT ST

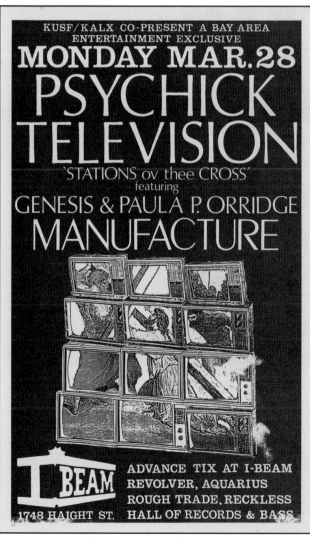

KUSF/KALX CO-PRESENT A BAY AREA
ENTERTAINMENT EXCLUSIVE
MONDAY MAR. 28
PSYCHICK TELEVISION
'STATIONS ov thee CROSS'
featuring
GENESIS & PAULA P. ORRIDGE
MANUFACTURE

I BEAM
1748 HAIGHT ST.

ADVANCE TIX AT I-BEAM
REVOLVER, AQUARIUS
ROUGH TRADE, RECKLESS
HALL OF RECORDS & BASS

HAVANA 3:00 AM

KENNEL CLUB
628 DIVISADERO

+ SPECIAL GUESTS
SAT. MAR. 6
$7.00 AT THE DOOR
DOORS OPEN 9:00
SHOWTIME 10:30
TICKETS AVAILABLE
AT BASS

SURF PARTY
WITH
AGENT ORANGE
THE WATCHMEN
S.J.'s FRONTLINE
LOVE NOODLE

SATURDAY, MARCH 26
MUSIC WORKS
2140 Market at Church
$7 at the door   9 PM
21 and over only
I.T.N. ROCK FOR THE 90's

psychedelic show

visuäl
Eyes of God

V.iS

FRIDAY SEPT. 6

The Tomb Of The Boy King

RECKLESS   CALENDAR magazine   WARD   KUSF 90.3

& THE KENNEL CLUB PRESENT:

TRASH!

PRE-WAR BERLIN PARTY

SURPRISES & SPECIAL GUEST GET DECADENT!

→ D.J. MICHAEL READ OF RECKLESS, SPINNING GLAM, GORE, PUNK & MORE
→ 2 FOR 1 JAGERMEISTER 9—11 P.M.,
→ FREE RECORDS AND POSTERS

KENNEL CLUB 628 DIVISADERO

TUESDAY, NOVEMBER 24
GATES OPEN 9:00
SHOWTIME 10:00
$3.00 AT THE DOOR

SO COME ON OUT AND REALLY DO SOMETHING!

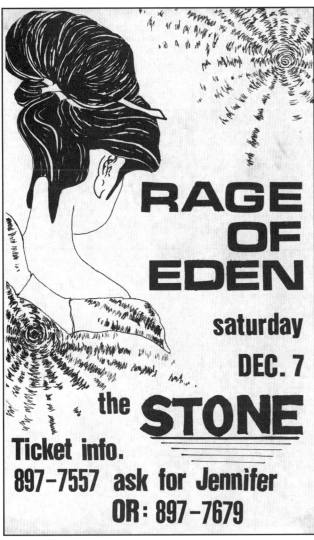

RAGE OF EDEN

saturday DEC. 7

the STONE

Ticket info.
897-7557 ask for Jennifer
OR: 897-7679

RECKLESS   CALENDAR magazine   WARD   KUSF 90.3

& THE KENNEL CLUB PRESENT:

TRASH!

Phantom Tollbooth

→ D.J. MICHAEL READ OF RECKLESS, SPINNING GLAM, GORE, PUNK & MORE
→ 2 FOR 1 JAGERMEISTER 9—11 P.M.
→ FREE RECORDS AND POSTERS

KENNEL CLUB 628 DIVISADERO

TUESDAY, NOVEMBER 10
GATES OPEN 9:00
SHOWTIME 10:00
$3.00 AT THE DOOR

SO COME ON OUT AND REALLY DO SOMETHING!

BUTTHOLE SURFERS
Tues. Nov. 3

BEAT NIGS
PLUS
THE FURIES
in the Upstairs Lounge
Tix $13
Door 8/Show 9

OLD Fillmore

Notes: Dinner served starting at 6pm. Minors welcome. Two drink minimum. Secure parking available in Fillmore Garage. Tickets at all BASS outlets including Tower and certain Wherehouse locations, and at Fillmore box office Tues-Friday from 11 'til 6. All tickets subject to service charge. The Fillmore is available for rental, call 771-2433. Doors open 8pm/ Show 9pm.

1807 Geary (at Fillmore)
Info: 567-2060

BUTTHOLE SURFERS

An Afternoon of SUSHI & SAKE
SEPT. 8
SUNDAY 4:30 pm

At the Nightbreak
1821 Haight
with
Palmetto State

Apearing At
© 628 Divisadero
567-0520
VIS
Night Club

THE
BY JOHN

and
LAWN
COMEDY

Saturday
JULY
12th

THREE DAY STUBBLE
from S.Houston Tx.
R.I.P.-88

lemony fresh
Schrödinger's Cat
CLEAN

Also from Santa Cruz
Rustleing Worms
PLUS Sally K.

PEOPLE'S THEATRE, FORT MASON, BLDG. B
JULY 11-27

RESERVATIONS AND INFORMATION 776-8999

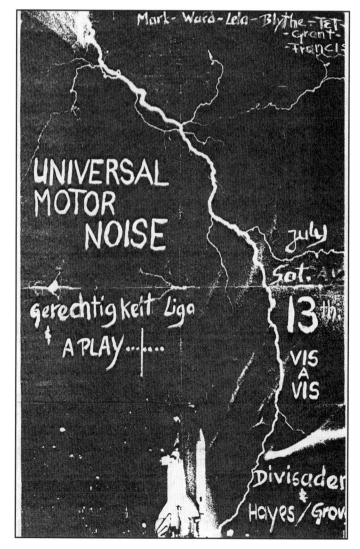

Mark-Ward-Lela-Blythe-Tet-Grant-Francis

UNIVERSAL MOTOR NOISE

Gerechtigkeit Liga
& A PLAY....+....

July
Sat.
13th

VIS
A
VIS

Divisader
&
Hayes/Grov

242

FAITH NO MORE
Thursday Aug. 14
at the STONE

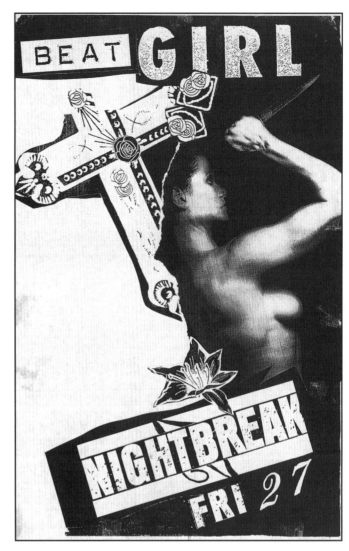

BEAT GIRL
NIGHTBREAK
FRI 27

MADNESS
LIVE!
THURSDAY
May 15TH
with
THE RHYTH-O-MATICS
THE FILLMORE
1805 Geary
All Shows 9 p.m.

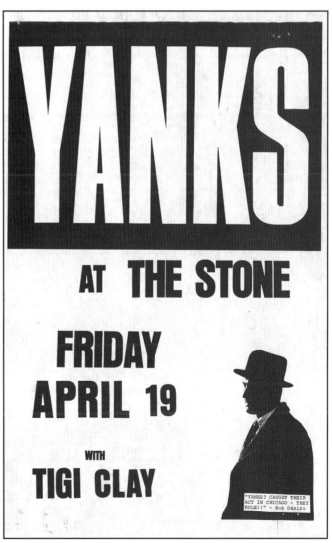

YANKS
AT THE STONE
FRIDAY
APRIL 19
with
TIGI CLAY

"YANKS? CAUGHT THEIR ACT IN CHICAGO - THEY RULE!!" - Bob Deniro

DEFECTORS Thurs
Sept. 19th
V.I.S. club
628 Divisadero (near McAllister.)

WHITE STAGG
BAND
AUG $3
21st wed
CLUB 9 PM
V.I.S. S.F.
628 DIVISADERO

SISTER DOUBLE HAPPINESS
2 BIG SHOWS! 2 BIG NIGHTS!
Thursday August 13th at
NIGHT BREAK
with *Pirates of Venus*
1821 Haight St 9:30 Prompt

Friday August 14th at the
CHATTERBOX
with the *Birdkillers*
853 Valencia 821-1891

NIGHTBREAK
DODGY BOILERS and 88 MAGIK
sat. Sept. 19

THE ESSENCE OF JACK
KEROUAC
A J·A·Z·Z P·L·A·Y

PIGLATIN
WHITEFRONTS

FREE
SUN. APRIL 13
4:00 PM
NIGHTBREAK

Reservations & Information: 647-8098
TICKETS: $7.00 & $9.00

Me Worry? No — I Got
Best in the West

JOE MAMA
IN MY FACE

D.I.S.C FRYDAY
THE 22nd
MCM & the MONSTER

NIGHTBREAK

HIGH-VOLTAGE HORROR
SPEEDWAY RECORDS
BIZARRE
NIGHTBREAK PRESENTS
1821 Haight 221-9008

LIONS AND GHOSTS
BLAM!

With Special Guests:

Chvnge
MAKES PEOPLE EXPLODE!

SAT. the 21ST
HAPPY 'ARMED FORCES DAY'!

TAKE advantage of prospects. Social life runs non-stop and new chums are generous. All weekend, insight helps you shed self-destructive habits. While working out inner conflicts, stress material goals as well.

SURGEON GENERAL'S WARNING: Drinking BEER Now Greatly Reduces Serious Risks to Your Health.

DANCE

CAN YOU BELIEVE IT?

FRI FREE MAY 9TH

BAD HABIT
CHANGELING
SEX FARM

APPEARING LIVE
AT THE
FABULOUS MABUHAY GARDENS
443 BROADWAY
10:00
SAN FRANCISCO

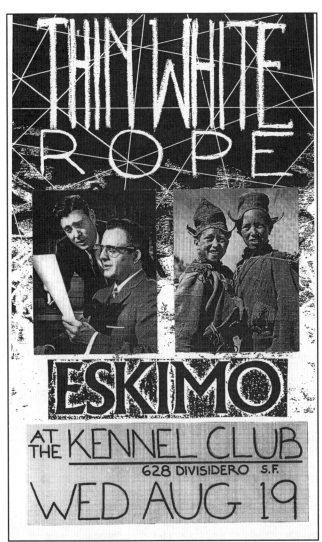

THIN WHITE ROPE

ESKIMO

AT THE KENNEL CLUB
628 DIVISIDERO S.F.
WED AUG 19

Celebrity Skin WITH BUCK NAKED AND THE BARE BOTTOM BOYS

San Francisco — Buy frightwig drinks at their Club Xomotion show Sat March 19 2779 16th St

ALSO DON'T BE LEFT OUT BUY Celebrity Skin t-shirts 10.00

Celebrity Skin
BUCK NAKED AND THE BARE BOTTOM BOYS

MARCH 24 THURSDAY

KENNEL CLUB
628 DIVISADERO

ALL AGES

STOP «« THAT »» TRAIN

AT THE STONE
412 BROADWAY

ALSO APPEARING........

BASIC RADIO
AND
CAPTURE THE FLAG

DOOR OPENS 7PM
SHOW AT 7:30
$5 COVER

««« THURS. JULY 24th »»»

INFORMATION 391-8282

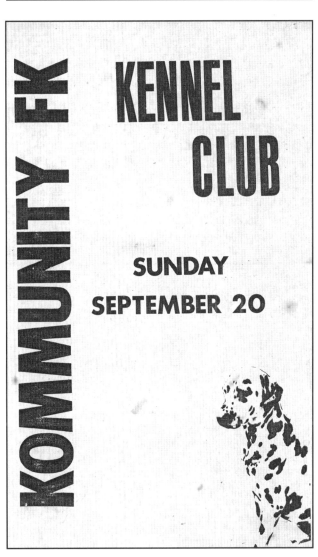

KOMMUNITY FK

KENNEL CLUB

SUNDAY
SEPTEMBER 20

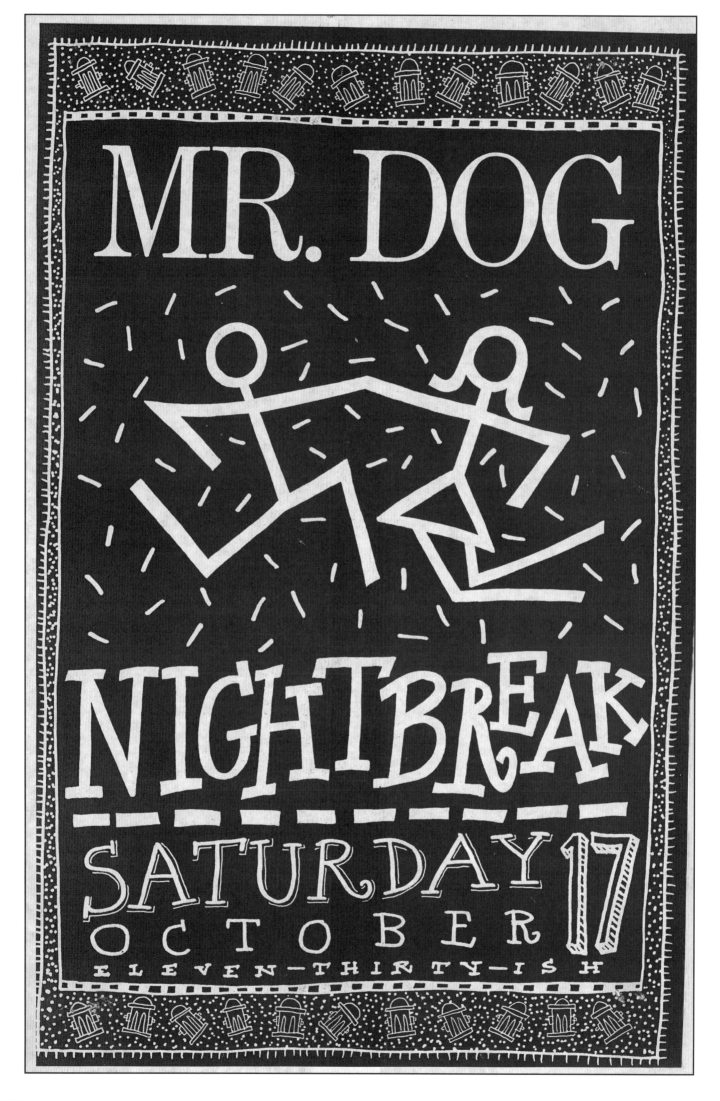

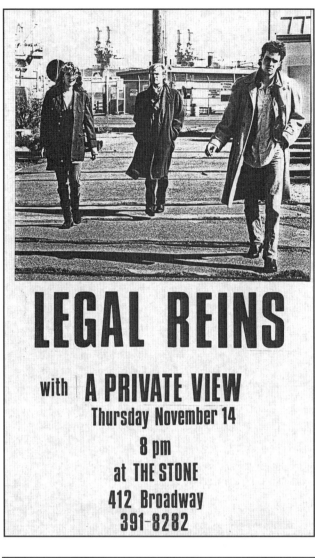

LEGAL REINS

with | A PRIVATE VIEW
Thursday November 14

8 pm

at THE STONE

412 Broadway

391-8282

THE STAND
WE DON'T WANT TO CHANGE THE WORLD...JUST HAUNT IT A LITTLE...

sunday, november 22nd
4:30 PM at the NIGHTBREAK · FREE

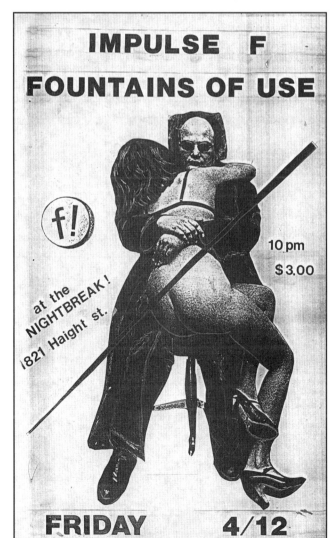

IMPULSE F
FOUNTAINS OF USE

f!

10 pm
$3.00

at the NIGHTBREAK!
1821 Haight st.

FRIDAY   **4/12**

MORALLY BANKRUPT
BAY AREA BLITZ!

SUNDAY 9/1
MARX MEADOW
GOLDEN GATE PARK

WITH: · FAITH NO MORE ·
· GLORIUS DIN ·
· THOUGHT FACTORY ·
· INFANT BOND OF JOY ·

TUESDAY 9/3
V.I.S. CLUB
DIVISADERO AT GROVE, S.F.

WITH: · DRUNK INJUNS ·
· TALES OF TERROR ·
· SHORT DOGS GROW ·
(BE SURE TO COME EARLY)

FRIDAY 9/6
RUTHIES INN
2618 SAN PABLO, BERKELEY

WITH: · FANG ·
· SACRILIDGE ·
· BONELESS ONES ·

BE THERE OR BE SQUARE

CALL- 863-7696 FOR DETAILS

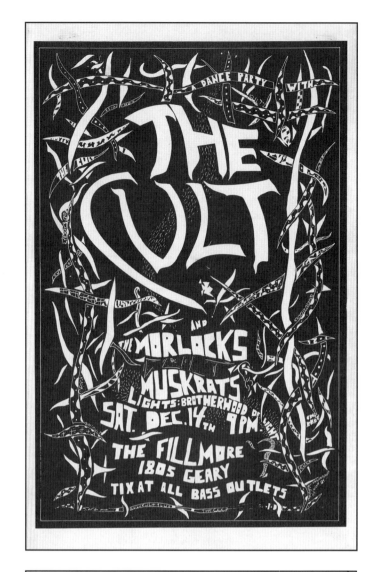

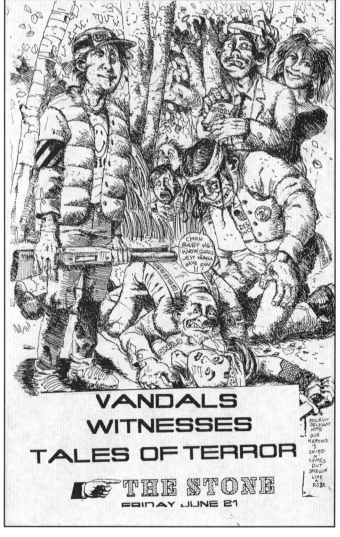

JANE STONE 8

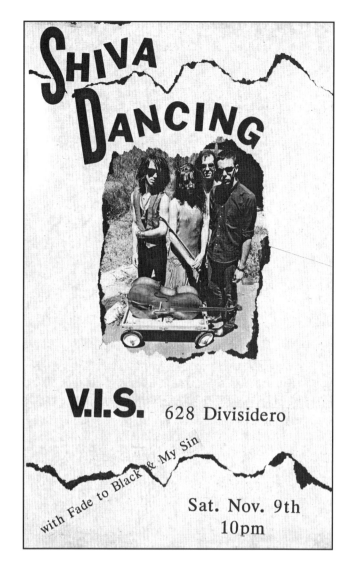

SHIVA DANCING

V.I.S. 628 Divisidero

with Fade to Black & My Sin

Sat. Nov. 9th
10pm

voluntary living

7-2 Tues.
V.I.S.
Club

7-7 Sun.
16th Note

PGR
BRICKMEN
FROM L.A. –
TUPELO CHAINSEX

VIS CLUB
JULY 17, '85
10:00 P.M.

$5 COVER

AfterHours

Gender Bender Offenders:
the Best MIX in Town!

Every Saturday starting February 1st (2am-dawn)
Dance mix with guest D.J.s plus good food. $5. cover.

baybrick inn   Entertainment information: 552-1121
683 Clementina (Baybrick's back door)

RECKLESS   CALENDAR magazine   WARD   KUSF 90.3x

& THE KENNEL CLUB PRESENT:

TRASH!

DETROIT SOUND

mc5 stooges b.o.c.

→→ D.J. MICHAEL READ OF RECKLESS,
SPINNING GLAM. GORE, PUNK & MORE
→→ 2 FOR 1 JAGERMEISTER 9–11 P.M.,
→→ FREE RECORDS AND POSTERS

KENNEL CLUB
628 DIVISADERO

TUESDAY, DECEMBER 1
GATES OPEN 9:00
SHOWTIME 10:00
$3.00 AT THE DOOR

SO COME ON OUT AND
REALLY DO SOMETHING!

the Kennel Club

WACKY
WEDS
JULY
15th

628 Divisadero St.   931-!9!4

ARE YOU EXPERIENCED?

Mr. T. Experience
Plus
the Sneetches

DOLLAR BOTTLES OF BUD $3 cov.

Sun 29
At
Night
Break

free
Music
4:00
pm

+ American English

THE VEIL RECORD RELEASE

4·27

NIGHTBREAK

BIRD KILLERS
Se2 HAGS
NIGHTBREAK 3:00 PM
SUN. APRIL 6.

NIGHTBREAK
SUSHI

Tell 'em Charlie sent you!

SUNDAY, APRIL 10
HALF BLIND
GASM
DJ JIM BO BOB   no cover

TUESDAY, APRIL 12
NOONDAY
UNDERGROUND
METRO
DJ BRAD   two dollars

1$ BEER

SPEEDWAY RECORDS

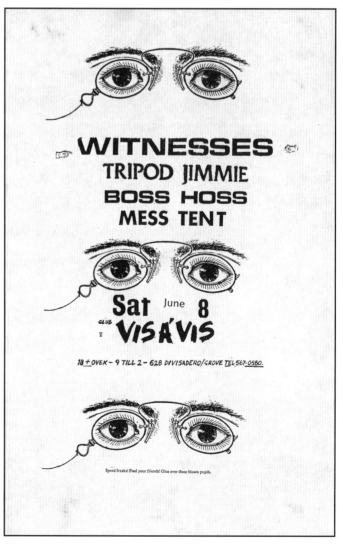

WITNESSES
TRIPOD JIMMIE
BOSS HOSS
MESS TENT

Sat June 8
CLUB
Y VIS A' VIS

18 + OVEK - 9 TILL 2 - 628 DIVISADERO/GROVE TEL 567-0560.

Speed freaks! Fool your friends! Glue over those blown pupils.

254

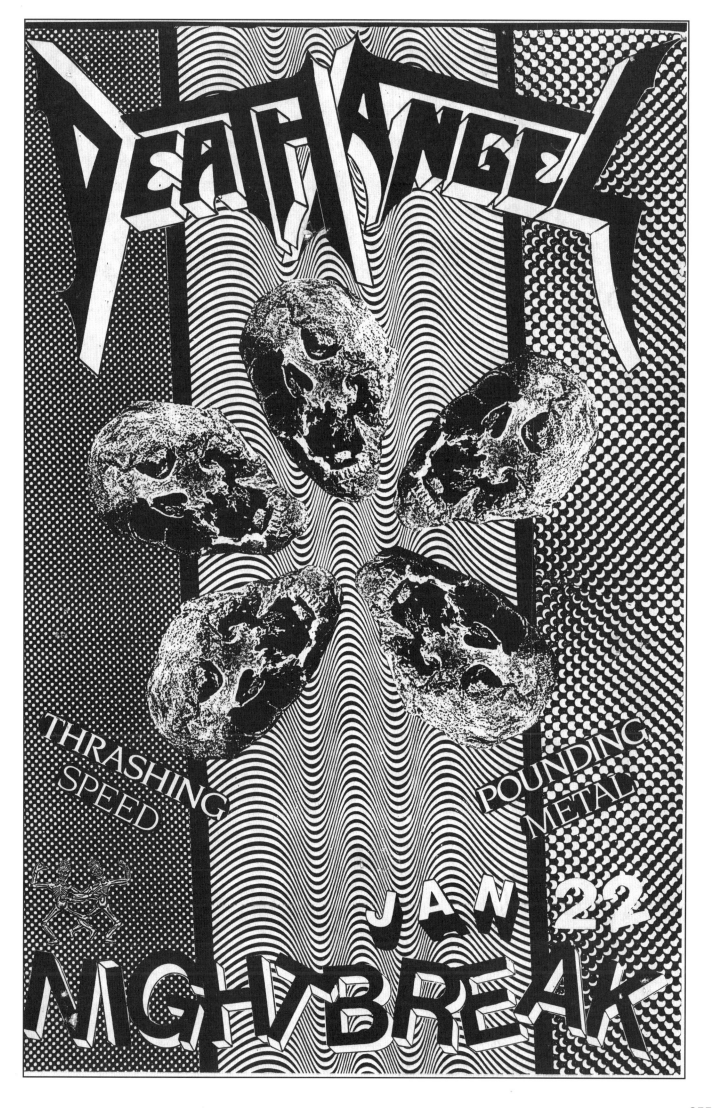

255

ESKIMO
AND BEATNIK BEATCH

AT THE KENNEL KLUB WED SEPTEMBER 14

the BIRD KILLERS
JACK WATERSON (of green on red)
vulgar & the Woodcutters
WED 10:00 NOV 4th
kennel Club
629 Divisadero

NIGHTBREAK
1821 HAIGHT ST. 221-9008
FRI. 4/1
BLACKBIRD
DIE BOSSA NOVA
SAT. 4/2
SCREAMING SIRENS
BUCK NAKED AND THE BARE BOTTOM BOYS
FRI. 4/8
SPANISH ELVIS
SAT. 4/9
SHIVA DANCING
SHE DEVILS
FRI. 4/15
THE NAKED INTO
SAT. 4/16
DEXTER DEVOE
FRI. 4/22
SURF M.C.'s
ONE TAKE JAKE
SAT. 4/23
MISSLE HARMONY
FRI. 4/29
MONKEY RHYTHM
SAT. 4/30
MR. DOG
BRING YOUR LP's, CD's TO SELL AND TRADE
SPEEDWAY RECORDS

Turkey on the run
FREE   FREE
Thee Hellhounds
SISTER DOUBLE HAPPINESS
BOHEMIAN LOVE JONES
I-BEAM
WEDNESDAY
NOVEMBER 25
PLEASE BRING CANNED FOOD
DONATIONS FOR ST. ANTHONY'S

256

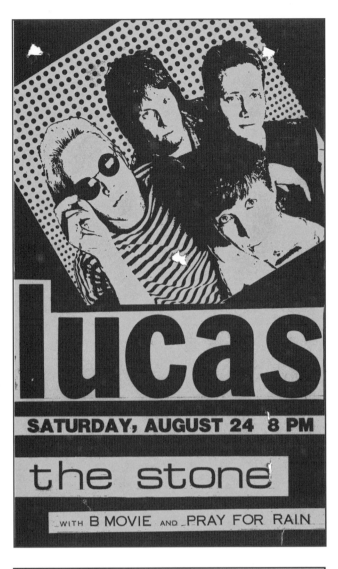

lucas

SATURDAY, AUGUST 24 8 PM

the stone

WITH B MOVIE AND PRAY FOR RAIN

Lyres
die kreuzen

MONDAY SEPT. 19

I-BEAM
1748 HAIGHT ST.

KUSF/KALX/KFJC CO-PRESENT
A SF EXCLUSIVE

ADVANCE TIX AT I-BEAM, AQUARIUS
REVOLVER, SPEEDWAY
ROUGH TRADE, RECKLESS
HALL OF RECORDS   762-BASS

BAY AREA EXCLUSIVE
FROM NEW YORK

THEY MIGHT BE GIANTS

CARMAIG de FOREST
FROM L.A.

KENNEL CLUB
628 DIVISADERO

SAT. MAR. 26
$7.00 AT THE DOOR
DOORS OPEN 9:00
SHOWTIME 10:30
TICKETS AVAILABLE
AT BASS

KUSF/KALX CO-PRESENT THE I-BEAM'S
XMAS PARTY
MONDAY DEC. 21
FREE ADMISSION
OUR XMAS GIFT TO YOU

THE SEAHAGS
FROM LA
THE HANGMEN
THE BIRDKILLERS
DEFINITELY NOT A SILENT NIGHT

I-BEAM
1748 HAIGHT ST.
DOORS 9pm

PLEASE BRING
TOY DONATION
FOR
'TOYS FOR TOTS'
OVER 21 PLEASE

257

ATA/PGR
Productions
presents:

NOISE
NACHT
1:
a reorganization of the sound spectrum

Poison Gas
RESEARCH

BIG CITY ORCHESTRA · THE FLYING NUNS
Nov. 2 10pm Martin Weber Gallery
220 8th & Howard · $3 donation · 431·8394
acoustic treatment by Leonard Marcel

THE STONE presents...

MACABE METAL
w/
NITEMARE

curfew
show
7pm

$5 all ages

plus
special guest
ENFORCER, & bLOODbAth

SAN FRANCISCO
THE STONE
OCT · 13 TH

NOFX

NO USE FOR A NAME
647-F
TERVEAT KADET
FINLAND
DROWNING ROSES
GERMANY

FRI AUG 17
924 GILMAN BERKELEY

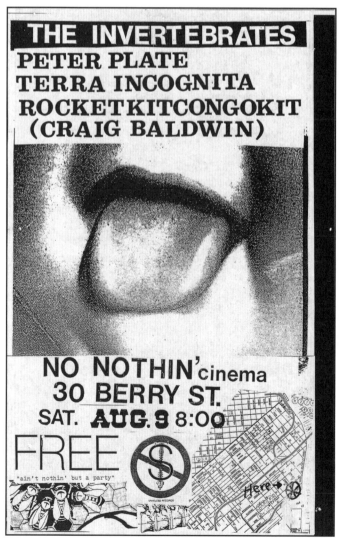

THE INVERTEBRATES
PETER PLATE
TERRA INCOGNITA
ROCKETKITCONGOKIT
(CRAIG BALDWIN)

NO NOTHIN' cinema
30 BERRY ST.
SAT. AUG. 9 8:00

FREE

"ain't nothin' but a party"

Here →

SVT
JUNE
FRIDAY 26TH

DAS BLOK
BERKELEY SQUARE
ELEMENTS OF STYLE

ROCK! AGAINST BOREDOM

SAM I AM
CORRUPTED MORALS
NOTHING SACRED
TOMMY ROT
DEFECTIVE YEAR
ECONOCHRIST
SKIN FLUTES
BIG BIG BIG

A benefit for 924 Gilman YOUR CLUB
SUNDAY APRIL 23RD
$4.00

STARTS 3:00 P.M.
ALL AGES WELCOME

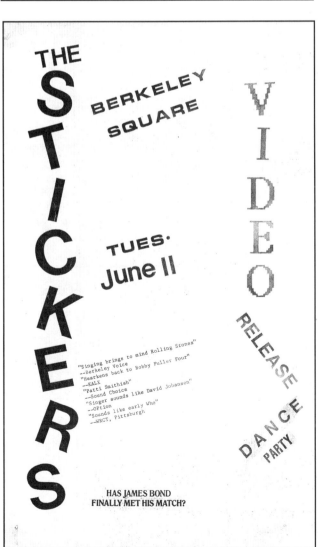

THE STICKERS

BERKELEY SQUARE

VIDEO

TUES. June 11

"Singing brings to mind Rolling Stones"
--Berkeley Voice
"Hearkens back to Bobby Fuller Four"
--KALX
"Patti Smithish"
--Sound Choice
"Singer sounds like David Johansen"
--Option
"Sounds like early Who"
--WRCT, Pittsburgh

RELEASE

DANCE PARTY

HAS JAMES BOND
FINALLY MET HIS MATCH?

BATTLE OF THE BANDS
924 GILMAN STREET

Surrogate Brains (Stockton)
TOMMY ROT (Oakland)
Mental Pygmies (Martinez)
SUBJECT to CHANGE (santa Rosa)
BLATZ (Pinole)
NOTHING'S SACRED (San Jose)
POLLUTION CIRCUS (Sacramento)
BOO HSS PHFFT!

SUNDAY, FEB. 5
3pm $4
ALL AGES NO ALCOHOL

SEA HAGS

NIGHTBREAK
thur

may 29

BIRD KILLER

NECROPOLIS/
OF LOVE

DJ DAVID BASSIN

Apr. 24
Thurs.

NIGHTBREAK

SIVA DANCING

thurs
jn
19

g.t. jesus

NIGHTBREAK

1821 Haight

NIGHTBReaK
1821 Haight 221-9008

SAT JULY 2 $4
door 9pm

TOOTH & NAIL

THE BELOVED

SPEEDWAY RECORDS

Halloween Party
with
WAGES OF SIN

SEA HAGS

and Silent Night

NOV 1 FRI 9:00

The Vis Club
628 divisadero

567-0660

JETBOY

GRAND OPENING OF
MABUHAY GARDENS
ON BROADWAY
435 Broadway, S.F.

SAT, JULY 13th

FROM L.A.
w/ DOLL
+ THE SEAHAGS

MON, JULY 15th AT THE VIS CLUB
638 DIVISIDERO · GROVE, S.F.
w/ THE SEA HAGS

LISTEN TO JETBOY INTERVIEW ON KUSF 90.3FM FRI JULY 12th 3 PM

DRESS TO KILL

JET BOY Info. Send self addressed stamped envelope to
P.O. Box 590868, S.F. CA 94159-0868
Modern Management

CHRIS ISAAK
SILVERTONE
AUG 26 - SAT AUG 30
NINE
FIVE NIGHTS

399 9th (Harrison) St
Gala Opening Party
Tuesday, Aug. 26, 10 p.m.

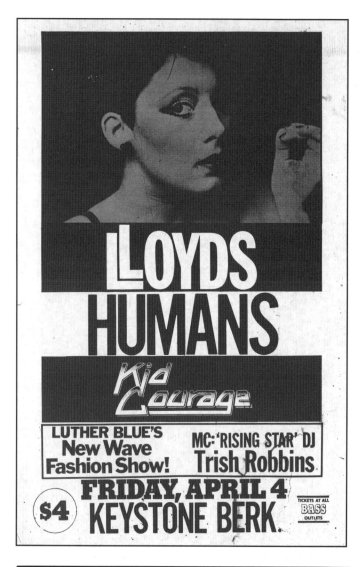

LLOYDS
HUMANS
Kid Courage
LUTHER BLUE'S
New Wave
Fashion Show!
MC: 'RISING STAR' DJ
Trish Robbins
$4
FRIDAY, APRIL 4
KEYSTONE BERK.
TICKETS AT ALL BASS OUTLETS

CHRIST ON PARADE
FINAL PERFORMANCE!

with
NEUROSIS
STEEL POLE BATH TUB
ECONOCHRIST
NUCLEAR ROACH

924 GILMAN SAT OCT 28

Nightbreak
Fri. May 16

11 pm

1821 Haight

1821 Haight

11 pm

Fri. May 16
Nightbreak

262

THE
NOISE SCOUTS

EVERYTHING
NOON DAY
UNDERGROUND

THURSDAY
MARCH 3 AT THE OMNI

DO A LOUD THING DAILY

VICTIMS
FAMILY

STICKDOG

RAINING HOUSE ——— CRIMP SHRINE
═══ ALL AGES ═══
SUNDAY FEB 28
GILMANPROJECT

TRIAL
— PERFORMS —
THE FRACTURED APPARATUS

— WITH —
A VARIATION OF THE DIDO AENEAS
SAT. JUNE 7 • 10:00 PM
— AT —
MEDIA
360 NINTH ST.
BTWN HARRISON AND FOLSOM, SF
$4   INFORMATION~864-0308

MUSIC & FILMS
THE INVERTEBRATES
& The BLEEDERS

NO NOTHIN' cinema
30 BERRY ST.
SAT. JUNE 14 8:00
FREE
"ain't nothin' but a party"
Here →

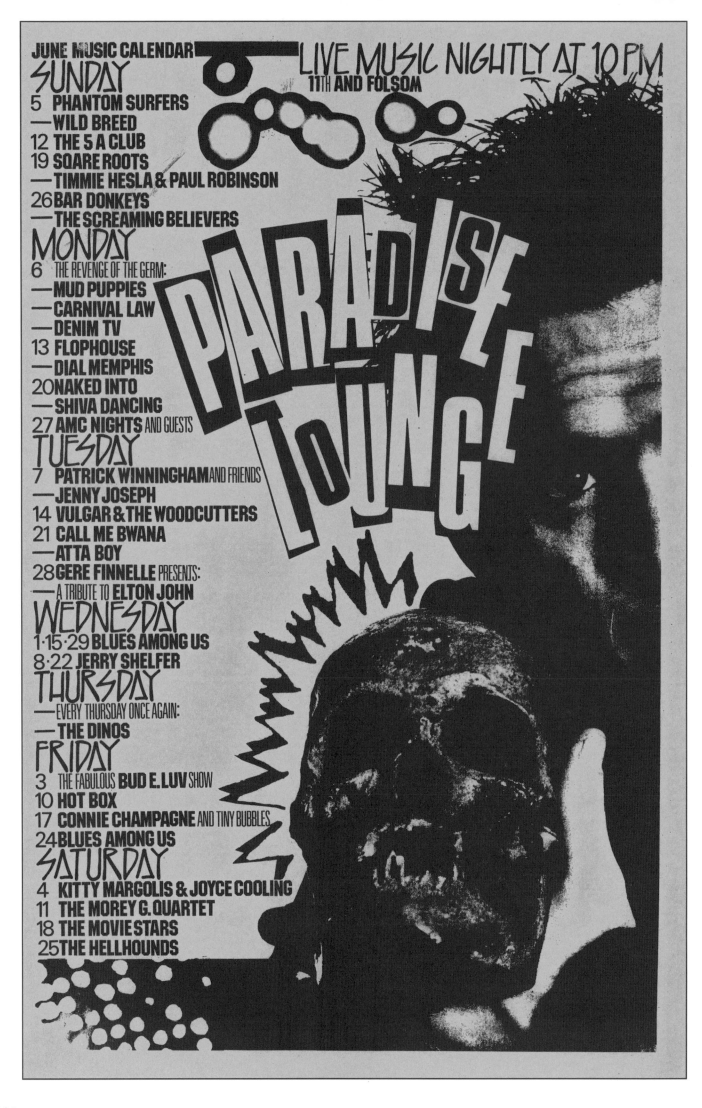

JUNE MUSIC CALENDAR

LIVE MUSIC NIGHTLY AT 10 P.M.
11TH AND FOLSOM

PARADISE LOUNGE

SUNDAY
5 PHANTOM SURFERS
— WILD BREED
12 THE 5 A CLUB
19 SQARE ROOTS
— TIMMIE HESLA & PAUL ROBINSON
26 BAR DONKEYS
— THE SCREAMING BELIEVERS

MONDAY
6 THE REVENGE OF THE GERM:
— MUD PUPPIES
— CARNIVAL LAW
— DENIM TV
13 FLOPHOUSE
— DIAL MEMPHIS
20 NAKED INTO
— SHIVA DANCING
27 AMC NIGHTS AND GUESTS

TUESDAY
7 PATRICK WINNINGHAM AND FRIENDS
— JENNY JOSEPH
14 VULGAR & THE WOODCUTTERS
21 CALL ME BWANA
— ATTA BOY
28 GERE FINNELLE PRESENTS:
— A TRIBUTE TO ELTON JOHN

WEDNESDAY
1·15·29 BLUES AMONG US
8·22 JERRY SHELFER

THURSDAY
— EVERY THURSDAY ONCE AGAIN:
— THE DINOS

FRIDAY
3 THE FABULOUS BUD E. LUV SHOW
10 HOT BOX
17 CONNIE CHAMPAGNE AND TINY BUBBLES
24 BLUES AMONG US

SATURDAY
4 KITTY MARGOLIS & JOYCE COOLING
11 THE MOREY G. QUARTET
18 THE MOVIE STARS
25 THE HELLHOUNDS

Fade To Black

MAJOR PONDS

THURS. NOV. 21

CRAWL AWAY MACHINE

"MAKE THE COLLECTOR NERD SWEAT" 10" COMPILATION RECORD RELEASE PARTY.

PLAID RETINA
THE OFFSPRING
MR. T EXPERIENCE
LOOKOUTS
COFFEE & DONUTS
CRUMMY MUSICIANS

ALSO ON THE RECORD:
JAWBREAKER
SAM I AM
the WRONG
CRIMPSHRINE

924 GILMAN ST. AT 8TH IN BERKELEY

Verysmall RECORDS

FRIDAY JAN 5

8 PM SHARP! 6 BANDS 6 BUCKS!

drawing by sergie, flyer by petey

FLESHIES
AND THE PHANTOM LIMBS
U.S. TOUR SEND OFF!!
WITH TOTIMOSHI
BIBLE OF THE DEVIL (Illinois)
FINKY BINKS : LoS RABBIS
in BERKELEY
SAT AUG 25th AT 924 GILMAN ST.

8:00 PM ALL AGES

ELBOWS AKIMBO

ASYLUM

MAY 7-8-9 THE LAB 1805 DIVISADERO 8:30pm $5

more info: 346-4063

the Quake presents FM99

Y·A·N·K·S

RECORD RELEASE

"MADE IN THE STATES"

FRIDAY
SEPT 28

THE STONE

WITH **VAUXHALL** AND **SNAPPERS**

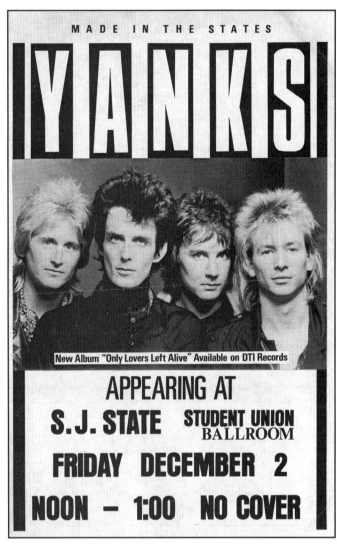

MADE IN THE STATES

YANKS

New Album "Only Lovers Left Alive" Available on DTI Records

APPEARING AT

S.J. STATE STUDENT UNION BALLROOM

FRIDAY DECEMBER 2

NOON – 1:00 NO COVER

CELEBRATE WASHINGTON'S BIRTHDAY

YANKS

Paul Zahl   Jack Johnson   Owen Masterson   Steve Aliment

SUNDAY FEB. 19

WITH **FLYING TIGERS**

AND **P.T. & THE PLEASERS**

KEYSTONE BERKELEY

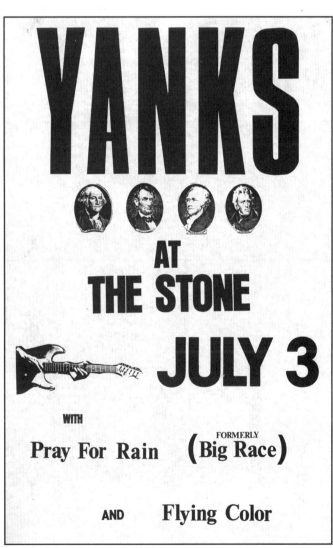

YANKS

AT THE STONE

JULY 3

WITH **Pray For Rain** (FORMERLY **Big Race**)

AND **Flying Color**

SAT. FEB.13TH at 2 THE CHI CHI / 11 PM

SOCIAL GODDESS

berkeley sq.

LUCAS 7/13

SEA★HAGS

SAT. MAY 2
MABUHAY
443 BROADWAY ST.

THELONIOUS MONSTER

THE McGUIRES

PROPER SHOES

431 1326

WIN TICKETS
ON KPOO 89.9 fm
wednesdays 3-6pm

THROW FOOD NOT BOMBS!

ISOCRACY *REUNION!*

NO NEUROSIS ALTERNATIVE

BOO HISS PHFFT!

MONSULA *EX TALLY HOE NUCLEAR ROACH*

FREE HOT DOGS

924 GILMAN BERKELEY
TUES JULY 4 4:00 $3

A HERE KITTY KITTY PRODUCTION · ALL AGES NO ALCOHOL

S. Cat-invited
FRIDAY May 15th Night time
Back by popular demand!

Schrödinger's Cat

Akousma · Gork

a surprise performance by: The Hyena Cabaret · The Web

924 Gilman (Berkeley)

info: 648-3561

People who choose to think for themselves are choosing

GAME THEORY

Here's why: Game Theory, peak of 'pop'

Scott Miller exhibits the kind of flair for lyrics and youthful wonder about the world around him that would have led critics a decade ago to employ the "new Dylan" tag.
Los Angeles Times

AUGUST 5 the STONE with the SMITHEREENS

AUGUST 6 the BERKELEY SQUARE with DADDY in his DEEP SLEEP

924 GILMAN BERKELEY JULY

FRI 6	SAT 7
BLAST AISLE NINE LIFELINE THIRD RAIL SCHERZO	**PENELOPE HOUSTON** ED HAINES. SUNDIALS KEVIN ARMYS' RUMMAGE SALE

IF YOU DISLIKED GWAR, YOU'LL HATE L.A.'S MESSCORE...

13	14
GREEN JELLO WHITE TRASH DEBUTANTES COMMRADES IN ARMS RICK STARR KILLER CRACK	**FUNGO MUNGO** SPRAWL PAULS' GOD CRINGER DISAURAPHUS *MEMBERSHIP MEETING 5PM*

20	21
BEN WEASALS NEW MOVIE "DISGUSTEEN" + DEMISE (WIS.) WARLOCK PINCHERS BLATZ · FILTH	**BIG DRILL CAR** LEFT INSANE G. WHIZ BIG MISTAKE (CT) PLATAPUS SCROUGE

27	28
BLAST OFFSPRING MEATWAGON SLAMBODIANS	**ANGRY SAMOANS** YARD TRAUMA MUMMIES AG'S · AK-47 *MEMBERSHIP MEETING 5PM*

GILMAN IS ALL AGES · NO ALCOHOL · VOLUNTEER RUN
SHOW UPDATES 525·9926 · BOOKING 524·8180
MEMBERSHIP CARDS $2/YR. COMING IN AUG NOFX
TOXIC REASONS NEGAZIONE MDC

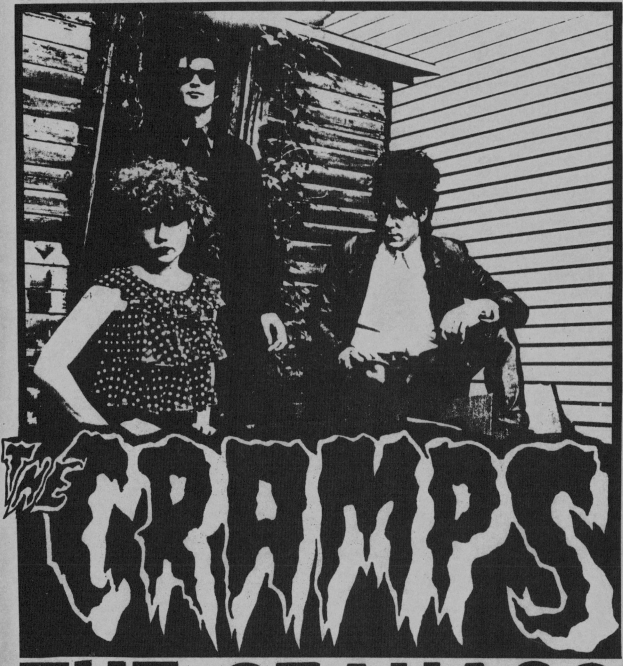

MON. & TUES. JULY 14 & 15
KUSF/ KALX CO-ANNOUNCE   BAY AREA EXCLUSIVE

THE CRAMPS

THE SEAHAGS
(MONDAY ONLY)

MONDAY :
DOORS OPEN 9:00   SHOWTIME 10:30

TUESDAY :
DOORS OPEN 7:30   SHOWTIME 9:00

ADVANCE TIX AT I BEAM
ROUGH TRADE, RECKLESS
REVOLVER, AQUARIUS
& DALJEETS

JULY 21-54-40

1748 HAIGHT ST

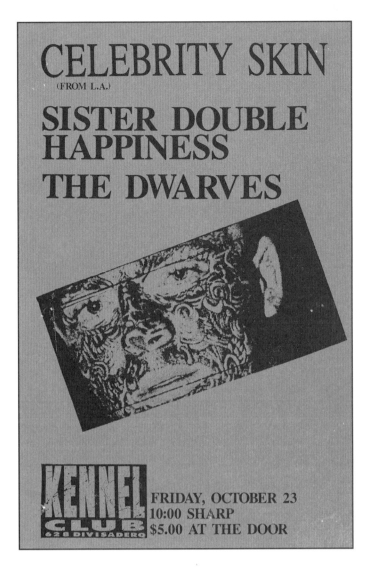

CELEBRITY SKIN
(FROM L.A.)

SISTER DOUBLE HAPPINESS

THE DWARVES

KENNEL CLUB
628 DIVISADERO

FRIDAY, OCTOBER 23
10:00 SHARP
$5.00 AT THE DOOR

NYMPHS   NIGHTBREAK
ALSO   FRI. JAN. 15

THE SEAHAGS

NIGHTBREAK
maximillions'

FRI., JAN. 29th
WITH
CHANGE

MUSIC FESTIVAL
All Day Festival – 12-7 pm
Holly Near
Arlo Guthrie
Sweet Honey in the Rock
Ronnie Gilbert
Inti-Illimani
Ferron
and the "Shadows on a Dime" Band
Linda Tillery
and Band
Judy Small

REDWOOD '85
RECORDS

GREEK THEATRE UC BERKELEY CA September 15

LORDS OF THE NEW CHURCH

Fade To Black

the black dolls

BERKELEY SQUARE

APRIL 30

doors open 9:00

GARY MYRICK AND THE TORTURE TWINS

10:00 p.m.
at SASCH

Tuesday June 14, 1988

11345 Ventura Blvd.
Studio City
(818) 7695555

McDisease McProfits

THE BEATNIGS

THE GILMAN STREET PROJECT 924 GILMAN @ 8TH, BERKELEY
NO VIOLENCE OR ALCOHOL $2 LIFETIME MEMBERSHIP

Clear & Distinct Ideas Presents

D.O.A.
THE DICKS
DIE KRUETZEN
POLKACIDE
FRIDAY DEC. 6
THE FARM
1499 POTRERO San Francisco

ALL AGES

Advance Tickets At:
BASS & ROUGH TRADE
INFORMATION; 431-1326

8:00 PM

ONLY OUTLAWS WILL HAVE SKATES

NORTH

POTRERO (47 VAN NESS BUS)

JAMES LICK FREEWAY

25th

THE FARM

ARMY

SKATERS' TOWN MEETING
@ THE FARM
1499 POTRERO
TUESDAY, SEPT 23
6:30 P.M.
Get rad,
BE THERE

FOR THE LATEST INFORMATION, CALL SHRED OF DIGNITY SKATERS UNION @ 863-7636

BEAT THE BAN
SUPERVISORS WANT TO BAN ALL SKATEBOARDS + SKATING IN THE CITY! YOURS NEXT?

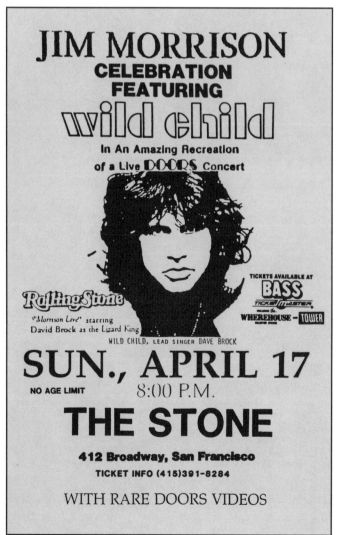

JIM MORRISON
CELEBRATION
FEATURING
wild child
In An Amazing Recreation
of a Live DOORS Concert

Rolling Stone
"Morrison Live" starring
David Brock as the Lizard King
WILD CHILD, Lead Singer DAVE BROCK

TICKETS AVAILABLE AT
BASS
TICKETMASTER
from the
WHEREHOUSE · TOWER

SUN., APRIL 17
NO AGE LIMIT 8:00 P.M.
THE STONE
412 Broadway, San Francisco
TICKET INFO (415)391-8284

WITH RARE DOORS VIDEOS

THE DNA LOUNGE PRESENTS
CAROL DODA

& her LUCKY STIFFS
SPECIAL GUEST M.C. **GREG KIHN**
THURSDAY SEPT 10 $5 admission
DOORS 9 SHOW 9:45
DNA LOUNGE 375 ELEVENTH ST
21+ID

ENIGMA RECORD RELEASE PARTY:

GAME THEORY
PLAN 9
RUSS TOLMAN
& THE TOTEM POLEMEN

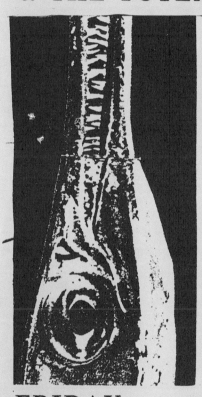

**FRIDAY,
OCTOBER 16
10:00 SHARP**

KENNEL
CLUB
628 DIVISADERO

SVT
ALIENS
friday oct*26th*9pm
RIO THEATER
799·0074

HIGHWAY 80 NORTH RODEO EXIT TO 140 PARKER
artbreakers

ROCK'N'ROLL MONSTER PARTY
SLOVENLY
BERKELEY SQUARE
Wed. Oct. 30

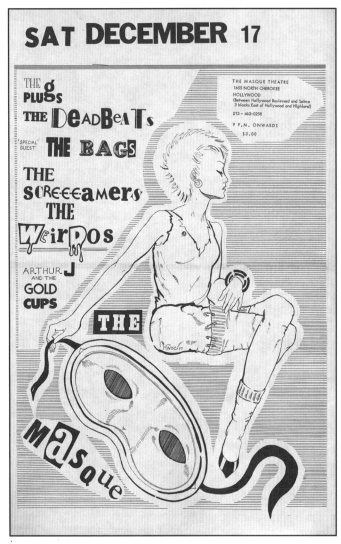

SAT DECEMBER 17

THE Plugs
THE DeadBeats
'SPECIAL' GUEST THE BAGS
THE SCREEEAMERS
THE WeirDos
ARTHUR J AND THE GOLD CUPS

THE MaSQUE

THE MASQUE THEATRE
1655 NORTH CHEROKEE
HOLLYWOOD
(Between Hollywood Boulevard and Selma
3 blocks East of Hollywood and Highland)
213 - 462-0258
9 P.M. ONWARDS
$3.00

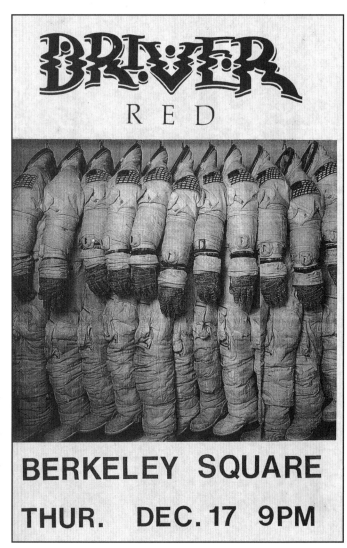

DRIVER RED
BERKELEY SQUARE
THUR. DEC. 17 9PM

NAOMI'S BACK!

MARIN
RANCHO
NICASIO
WED JAN 17

Naomi Ruth Eisenberg
band

FEATURING ROCKETTE MORTON
EX-CAPTAIN BEEFHEART'S MAGIC BAND

fotograph: w. schoppe foto hilfer: j. schoppe spielplatz bie Rose und Thistle mit
reklame: l. ogron friseur: s. saizan die Idols, 31. dezember $2.50

. . . . . . nelson randolph .. scott herron .. larry elliot .. jackie flatt .. mark blake . . . .

KID COURAGE

WORLD'S CUTEST KILLERS'

Kathy Valentine formerly of the Go-Go's
&
Members of Girlschool,
PIL and Broken Homes
LIVE AT THE FENCING CENTER

April 25th SAT.
Tickets $ 7.50 9 PM

40 N. 1st. S.J.

SAPPHIRE

THIS THURSDAY

DEC. 5   10:00 PM

THE CHI CHI CLUB

440 BROADWAY

NIGHTBReaK
1821 Haight 221-9008

tues. 22 sept.
3 BANDS
DOLLAR BEER

HOUSE OF WHEELS
RADICAL PUPPIES
RAZERS

wednesday 23
TOUCH ME
HOOKER

thursday 24
BLACKLIGHT
CHAMELEONS
LAWN VULTURES
SEAHAGS

friday 25
HOLY SISTERS OF GAGA DADA
CATHEADS

saturday 26 **77's**

JÖKÖ LIVE FRÖM TOKYO

ALSO:
THE PODS
BRUCE POLLACK
PHILIP HUYSER
TONY LABAT
KAREN FINLEY
TODD PLANTEEN

SAVOY
NOV. 6 THURS.

butt love
at **NIGHTBREAK**

Don't You Love...
Human Denial, Risk-taking

Don't You Love...
FANTASIES?

Just One More Thing......
When All Else Fails...
SHARE SOME SWEAT WITH

SAT., JAN. 30th

WITH **THEE HELLHOUNDS**

Let Your Erotic Imagination Run Rampant!

BUCK NAKED
AND THE BARE BOTTOM BOYS

The right choice.

because quality matters.

FROM AUSTIN, TEXAS
BAY AREA EXCLUSIVE

DINO LEE
& THE WHITE TRASH REVUE

KENNEL CLUB
628 DIVISADERO

MAXIMILLIONS M.C.

THURSDAY,
OCTOBER 29
DOORS OPEN 9:00
SHOWTIME 10:00
$6.00 AT THE DOOR

THE STAND

BRING ON THE WINTER OF LOVE...

FRIDAY DECEMBER 11th 9:00 at The Twilight Zone 2132 CENTRAL AVE ALAMEDA

THE ALBATROSS
(1608 WARREN STREET: IN UNIVERSITY SQUARE)
—MANKATO, MN.—
PRESENTS
AN ALL AGE HOLIDAY BASH
KATO'S OWN:

'Tis THE SEASON you Schmuck!

LIBIDO BOYZ

GRINCH

WITH from Minneapolis

BABES IN TOYLAND

THE FUN STARTS AT 7:30pm, BE THERE
$6.00 AT THE DOOR
FREE SODA BAR ALL NIGHT!

DECEMBER 20TH

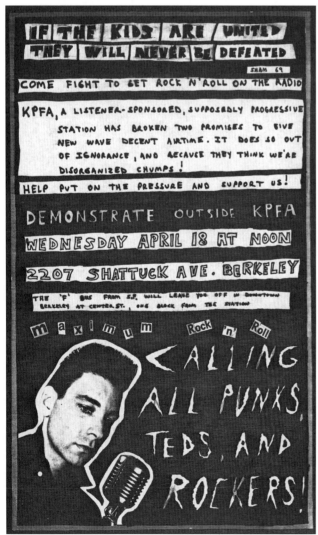

IF THE KIDS ARE UNITED THEY WILL NEVER BE DEFEATED
SHAM 69

COME FIGHT TO GET ROCK N' ROLL ON THE RADIO

KPFA, A LISTENER-SPONSORED, SUPPOSEDLY PROGRESSIVE STATION HAS BROKEN TWO PROMISES TO GIVE NEW WAVE DECENT AIRTIME. IT DOES SO OUT OF IGNORANCE, AND BECAUSE THEY THINK WE'RE DISORGANIZED CHUMPS!

HELP PUT ON THE PRESSURE AND SUPPORT US!

DEMONSTRATE OUTSIDE KPFA

WEDNESDAY APRIL 18 AT NOON

2207 SHATTUCK AVE. BERKELEY

THE 'F' BUS FROM S.F. WILL LEAVE YOU OFF IN DOWNTOWN BERKELEY AT CENTER ST. ONE BLOCK FROM THE STATION

maximum Rock n' Roll

CALLING ALL PUNKS, TEDS, AND ROCKERS!

DISCHARGE from ENGLAND   D.O.A
A-list   BAD BRAINS vs LEWD

SOCIAL UNREST

THE FARTZ

at the OAKLAND AUDITORIUM
ARENA DANCE FLOOR
FRI. OCT. 1   9:00pm
BASS   tickets available at bass

麗　晶

Regent Cafe

RESTAURANT • BAR • DANCING
952 CLEMENT ST. • SAN FRANCISCO
752-0354

每逢星期一、二晚 10PM—2AM

情調高尚
氣氛浪漫

金曲
勁舞
渡
良宵

熊貓隊

THE Pandas
PROFESSIONAL SOUND and LIGHTING

NEW WAVE DISCO DANCE BAND

The San Jose Invasion

Featuring:

kooch baHar   the endmen

Panda Mania   LONDON DOWN

Sunday, 8 November, 1987
The Kennel Club
628 Divisidero
San Francisco, CA
415-931-1914
$3.00   21 & over
Early Show - 5:00 PM

This isn't art this is suicide...

International Talent Network PRESENTS

BAD RELIGION

L.A.'s Finest

Congress runs your daily life but they brainwash You so you think it's freedom!!

Wave had a war every 20 years they make you think we really need them!

PLUS...

SHORT DOGS GROW

THE S.F. MUSIC WORKS

Sunday, January 24

DON'T

CALL CLUB FOR MORE INFO

8 O'Clock
5 Dollars

AND TUNNEL CREEPS

PLUS OTHER STRANGE EVENTS I'M SURE.

21 & OVER W/ I.D.

THE GOVORNMENT YOU VOTE FOR IS THE ONE THAT YOU POSESS

The VIS

628 DIVISADERO   567-0520

THE DEAD MILKMEN

Wed. Nov 19

9PM $4

EAT YOUR PAISLEY!

WITH THE MR. T EXPERIENCE

THE PSYCHEDELIC FURS
BOOK OF DAYS

NEW YEAR'S EVE

PLUS SPECIAL GUEST
EAST OF EDEN

BERKELEY COMMUNITY THEATRE • 9PM

SUNDAY DECEMBER 31

Live 105 *Modern Rock*

IN ASSN WITH

**TICKETS AVAILABLE AT ALL BASS TICKET CENTERS
INCLUDING TOWER RECORDS AND SELECTED WHEREHOUSE
HOME ENTERTAINMENT STORES. VISA/MC. SERVICE CHARGE.**

BASS TICKETS   CHARGE BY PHONE: 415/762-BASS • 408/998-BASS

Miller Genuine Draft
TAP INTO THE COLD

BILL GRAHAM PRESENTS

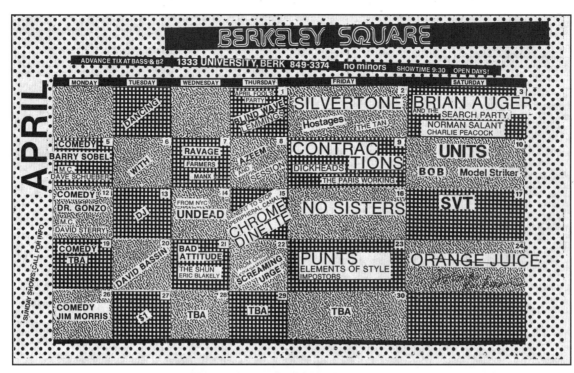

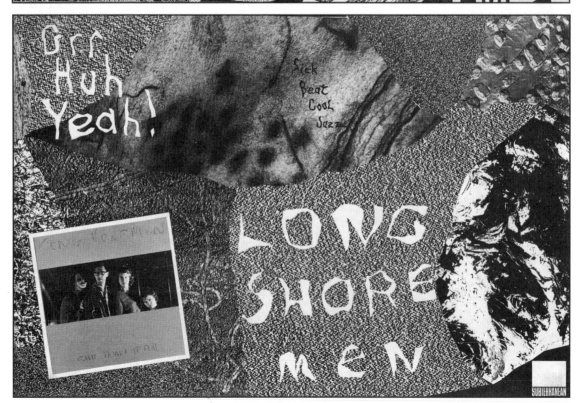